Coppola's hard-won sixty years of wisdom about writing, directing, actors, rehearsals, and groundbreaking technique, and his visionary hopes for the cinematic language." —Walter Murch

"Invoking intimate details of his childhood, some that he's never shared before, Coppola conjures up the magic world of television in the 1950s. Readers interested in the new technology will find this an eminently user-friendly book, but it is also peppered with brilliant personal observations about the most basic principles and techniques of filmmaking that will also fascinate readers who have no interest in making live cinema but simply loved *The Godfather*." —Wendy Doniger, author of *The Ring of Truth: And Other Myths of Sex and Jewelry*

"Coppola's natural abilities as a storyteller, regardless of the medium, are evident here. Sections dealing with his relationship to the prehistory of live cinema are as personally revealing as they are fascinating. . . . This consummate filmmaker's enthusiasm for cinema is infectious." —*Publishers Weekly*

"A curious and exhilarating account of a master in his field wrestling with a new way to convey his vision. The book begins with an exploration into the history of television in its infancy, when nearly every program was brought to audiences live, and it is peppered throughout with personal asides about how this technique has dogged his entire career. . . . As in his films, Coppola knows how to tell a compelling story. Live cinema, in its new incarnation, and everyone it attracts, will benefit from his insights." —Michael Ruzicka, *Booklist*

ALSO BY FRANCIS FORD COPPOLA

The Godfather Notebook

LIVE CINEMA

AND ITS TECHNIQUES

FRANCIS FORD COPPOLA

Liveright Publishing Corporation
A Division of W. W. Norton & Company
Independent Publishers Since 1923
New York London

For information about permission to reproduce selections from this book, write to
Permissions, Liveright Publishing Corporation, a division of
W. W. Norton & Company, Inc., 500 Fifth Avenue, New York, NY 10110

For information about special discounts for bulk purchases, please contact
W. W. Norton Special Sales at specialsales@wwnorton.com or 800-233-4830

Manufacturing by LSC Communications, Harrisonburg
Book design by JAMdesign
Production manager: Julia Druskin

ISBN 978-1-63149-454-3 pbk.

Liveright Publishing Corporation
500 Fifth Avenue, New York, N.Y. 10110
www.wwnorton.com

W. W. Norton & Company Ltd.
15 Carlisle Street, London W1D 3BS

1 2 3 4 5 6 7 8 9 0

TO JOHN FRANKENHEIMER

THE PIONEER

CONTENTS

Preface Why This Book   xi

Personal Introduction   1

1 Proof-of-Concept Workshops   5

2 A Short History of Film and Television   18

3 The Actors, Acting, and Rehearsal   33

4 Equipment and Technical Specifications   43

5 Scenery and Location   48

6 The Shame of Things to Come: Madison, Wisconsin   63

7 *One from the Heart*: Its Lessons   69

8 Rip Van Winkle   78

9 The Question of Style in the Cinema   81

10 The Stumble-Throughs, Technical Rehearsals, and
   Dress Rehearsals 92

11 Marks and Other Smaller Unresolved Problems   98

12 Obstacles and Other Thoughts on Live Cinema No Matter
   What They May Be   103

13 Equipment—Now and in the Near Future   106

Afterword Why Am I Doing This?   115

Appendix Journal Notes During OCCC Live Cinema
Production: May/June 2015   121

Glossary   159

Credits of the Live Broadcasts   165

Acknowledgments   191

Index   193

WHY THIS BOOK

Since the early 1990s, the cinema has transformed itself from a photochemical-mechanical medium to an electronic-digital one. It is a revolutionary process that seems to have just happened, but it actually occurred in small increments, the transition beginning in sound, then in editing, then digital cinematography, and finally, theatrical projection. The cinema is now just about wholly digital. Yet our love and respect for film masterpieces, from the silent era through the era of "talkies" and beyond, including extraordinary cinematic work around the globe, inspires us to make our new electronic cinema do little more than emulate the films of the past.

Many young filmmakers are loathe to abandon film, not realizing that it has already abandoned them. The Eastman Kodak factory in Rochester, New York, that used to employ over 3500 workers is now down to 350 as the need for Kodak film has shrunk to accommodate those few filmmakers (my own daughter Sofia one of them) who prefer working the old way. This inclination to use film is touching and totally understandable. Film and its traditions remain beloved. There even remain still photographers who make their own glass plates with emulsion of silver halides, as the results are so beautiful. No doubt there will always be a few passionate souls who will try to create photochemical film after none is manufactured. But the unalterable fact confronts us that cinema is now primarily an electronic-digital medium.

I have to believe that this change will profoundly influence the essence of the cinema, no matter how much we revere those many great works made on photographic film, taking us in new directions. What will these new directions be?

In the digital world, moviemaking can now be performed by directors collaborating on the internet, using game pads, joysticks, keyboards, and touch screens, all the devices of internet gaming. They can engage in play across geographical boundaries, perhaps even viewed by large audiences in auditoriums. And they can engage in role-playing games, identifying with and controlling individual characters and at the same time helping to create the defined worlds that are the settings. Virtual reality, with its point-of-view perception of the main characters, may create new formats; and movies themselves may be performed live, shown at theaters, in community centers, and in homes around the world. Eventually "cinema auteurs" may emerge who can use this format to create literature at its highest level, in ways I cannot yet imagine.

Of course, we have lived with live television since television was first invented—in fact, television was dominated by live programming until well into the 1950s and the development of videotape technology. But my own interest, Live Cinema, has only just appeared in this second decade of the twenty-first century. The purpose of this book is not to indulge in nostalgia, whether for live television or for the early days of filmmaking, but to explore this new medium, to discover how it is different from other creative forms, what its virtues and requirements are; and especially, to look at how it can be used and taught.

In its essence this new medium *is* cinema, not a television play, but conceived as cinema and yet not losing the thrill of a living performance. Thinking about all of the implications, I wanted to learn more—not just by talking about what Live Cinema might be, but by actually doing it. So I launched two experimental proof-of-concept workshops, one in the facilities of Oklahoma City Community College in 2015, and another a year later at UCLA's School of Theater, Film and Television. I learned a great deal from both workshops— my journal from OCCC is included in the appendix, followed by credits from both workshops—and, brimming over with knowledge and facts that I really hadn't digested, I decided to write them down in a user-friendly book. This is that book.

What you are about to read then is a manual, a guide through the many intricate issues one confronts when attempting to do a Live Cinema performance, from the all-important matters of the actors and how to rehearse them to the details of making use of sophisticated technology that was originally invented for television sports. Of course it is my dream to one day do a major Live Cinema production based on my own writing, but should the many reasons I cannot do this prevail, I hope that those who come after me will read this record of what I have learned from my Live Cinema workshops, and use it to work in this new art form.

PERSONAL INTRODUCTION

Born in 1939 and being as a child of a scientific leaning, I was drawn to and fascinated by the new wonder of my time, television. My father, who was a classical musician and first-chair flutist in the Toscanini NBC Symphony Orchestra, was also fascinated by innovation. He was the son of a master tool and die maker who had engineered and built the Vitaphone, the machine that made movies talk. In my earliest memories, my father was always bringing home the latest devices from the shops along New York City's "Radio Row": the Presto home acetate recorder, the wire and tape recorder, and then the first television set. I was seven, the perfect age to operate these things, so when our small-screen Motorola TV showed up in our Long Island home, I was in heaven.

True, in 1946 there was hardly any programming, so I spent hours watching the geometric test patterns, waiting for something to begin. I can remember the early shows. *Howdy Doody* looked nothing like the famous puppet in later years; he was then a lanky hayseed with blond hair whose face became wrapped in bandages because he was running for President, we were told, and had gone through plastic surgery. Of course, we kids knew nothing of the copyright suit going on, when the creator of the puppet refused to cede the rights to his character, and a new puppet design, this one with rights intact, had to be introduced to the audience. There were a few Allied Artists cowboy movies coming over on Channel 13 from New Jersey, and the DuMont Television Network offered shows on Channel 5, including *Captain Video and His Video Rangers*. When I was nine years old, I was paralyzed from polio. I became a prisoner in my room with the television my focus, along with some puppets, a tape recorder, and a toy 16mm movie projector. For a year I saw no children other than my brother and sister. With pleasure and longing, I watched the Horn and Hardart's *Children's Hour*, where talented children performed, and the most gorgeous little girls in the world sang and danced.

Later, as I grew and regained the ability to walk, I persisted in watching. By the age of 15, beguiled by the beautiful Golden Age of Television, I began to think I could write plays. This was a period known for its live, televised dramas: shows like the *Philco Television Playhouse* and *Playhouse 90*, featuring original dramas by young writers like Rod Serling and Paddy Chayefsky, and young directors like Arthur Penn, Sidney Lumet, and John Frankenheimer. Stunning and ambitious works like *Marty, Days of Wine and Roses*, and *Requiem for a Heavyweight* were performed live in those years before video tape recording, with stars like Ernest Borgnine, Jack Palance, Piper Laurie, and Cloris Leachman. (Many of these plays for television would soon be made into films.) Even as a teenager, I could see that some of these impressive productions seemed like movies in their style and their use of strong shots and cinematic expression; and without exception, the best of those were the work of John Frankenheimer, who later became a successful film director with many great films under his belt. I'd say that my notion of Live Cinema was hatched while watching Frankenheimer's work in live television, and something of that work remains with me to this day.

What I hope to accomplish in this book is to lay out the idea of Live Cinema and explore its techniques, as well as its possible benefits and apparent limitations. My perspective is that of a director who grew up on live television; who had early training in the theater; and who has spent a lifetime working as a screenwriter, producer, and director of movies. I have long dreamt of working in all these ways at once: in some form of Live Cinema. The technology continues to change, providing new answers to the questions "What for?" and "Why give up control?" How does Live Cinema differ from theater, television, and conventional cinema? Much of what I will discuss here was learned through intense personal reflection, and during two experimental workshops which involved using sections of my work in progress, a long (screen) play entitled *Dark Electric Vision*.

1

PROOF-OF-CONCEPT
WORKSHOPS

After several actor readings of my script I decided to do something more like a staged reading. This process evolved into phases of trying to perform sections of the story that would be performed live, and broadcast to some select theaters for viewing. When I made the decision to do a workshop to explore the possibility of Live Cinema, my original thought was to find a place where repertory actors might be available to "try out" some pages of my script, perhaps with some modest staging. I quickly learned that repertory actors are very busy and over-scheduled. I considered Austin, Texas, a city with some production activity, where I could go and try out ideas in some privacy. But local film production was ongoing, and most resources there were already well booked. Then I thought of Oklahoma City Community College (OCCC), where a long-time associate of mine, Gray Frederickson, was on the faculty.

Gray had previously asked me to speak there in order to help raise money for a new facility. The idea eventually emerged to conduct a class during which we'd try out some 50 or so pages of my script, and cast with local Oklahoma City repertory actors in a workshop.

Plan in hand, I arrived in Oklahoma City on April 10, 2015. I did the preliminary local casting, which included some actors from nearby Dallas. I prepared some 70 OCCC students in the various crew positions, and came back in May and spent six weeks there on the project, rehearsing, experimenting with sets and cameras, and eventually broadcasting a live performance to a number of private screening rooms. I learned so much during this time that about a year later I wanted to do a second workshop, to add new areas of learning. These were some of my new concerns:

1. Could I integrate large numbers of costumed extras into scenes shot in one day, augmenting them to principal actors and using EVS machines? (I'm going to mention the EVS a lot, otherwise known in slang as the "ELVIS," which is an amazing machine, technically a replay server.)
2. Could I create shots in camera by using lightweight scenic panels and props rather than stage on sets and props as is done normally?
3. Could I play scenes in Italian dialect, with subtitles that are dynamic and expressive on different places in frame and different sizes?
4. Could I end with a spectacular live stunt?
5. Could I smoothly switch between live cameras and camera shots previously recorded on EVS?

I knew that if I could come up with answers to these questions, the second experimental workshop would be a success and worth the money and effort it would take.

THE BASIC UNIT

Often, an artistic discipline has a BASIC UNIT out of which the whole is built. In prose literature, and really all writing, be it journalism or the novel, the basic unit is the sentence. If you have a great sentence, and it is followed by others that result in a great paragraph, joined by other paragraphs building up to yield a great chapter, you're on the way to a great book. In my OCCC workshop, I learned that in Live Cinema as in conventional cinema, the basic unit of the cinema is the shot. Shots tell the story. As we have learned from the silent film era, a shot can be a short component within a structure of shots that are then cut together in order to provide a great sequence. Or it can be long and complex, and tell much of the story itself, as in a Yasujiro Ozu film, or its opposite, a Max Ophuls film shot with extensive camera movement.

"A shot can be a word, but it's better when it's a sentence." For many years, I've had notes I'd written pinned up above my work area on a bulletin board marked "FC NOTES ON STORY AND CHARACTER."

1. *Character is revealed by behavior.*
2. *A story can be told through unique moments between its principal characters.*
3. *The memorable moment is often unspoken.*
4. *Something needs to happen.*
5. *Emotion. Passion. Surprise. Awe.*
6. *The shot can be a word, but it's better when it's a sentence.*
7. *Audiences want to become involved with the characters, want that involvement developed.*
8. *Beware of the cliché, the predictable.*
9. *Audiences want themselves and their lives explained and illuminated.*

In a recent phone call, my daughter Sofia told me she also had my same list pinned up, and she asked, "What does it mean the shot can be a word but it's better when it's a sentence?" In trying to remember what I had meant, I had to remind her (and myself) of two extreme poles of the concept of the "shot," these being films made by Ophuls and Ozu. Ozu (1903–1963) was a film director and screenwriter working throughout his lifetime in the Japanese cinema. In his long career, during which he turned from comedies to serious films, he had a unique style: his camera rarely if ever moved, and he held a beautifully composed shot for the duration of the scene. This lack of camera movement made each entrance and exit of characters very dynamic, as they moved in and out of the frame from left to right, right to left, back to front, front to back. Every shot in an Ozu film is a unit of importance, like a brick in a beautiful masonry wall. Max Ophuls (1902–1957), by contrast, used a style in which the camera almost never stopped moving. A German-born director working in Germany, France, and the United States, he was well known by the short poem written by actor James Mason:

> A *shot that does not call for tracks*
> *Is agony for poor old Max.*

Pure and simple, these two opposing cinematic styles came home to me early in my career, as I was caught between the disparate styles of two of the world's greatest cinematographers, Gordon Willis (*The Godfather*) and Vittorio Storaro (*Apocalypse Now*). I learned well. For the classic style used in *The Godfather*, each shot was meant as a brick in the structure of the scene, which then became a design of a great wall of bricks. One should never, according to Willis, include everything in the shot, or else there'd be no reason to cut to the next shot. The overall effect was created by the placement of each shot in relation to the next. Storaro, on the other hand, wished the camera to be used as a moving pen, gliding from element to element in *Apocalypse Now*.

What I finally explained to Sofia (and myself) was that the shot could be like a word, in that it expresses a simple idea: for example, in a "shot of town hall" the word means "here." Or it could be like a sentence: a shot of town hall, with the shadow of a lynched man cast upon it, could be read as "Here, justice is often abused."

THE LANGUAGE OF LIVE CINEMA

So, in cinema the basic unit is the *shot*, as in theater the basic unit is the *scene*. In television the basic unit is the *event*. Whether for a sporting event or a live television play, one is forced to get what shots one can to cover the event. In cinema, on the other hand, we carefully design not only the shot but the magical effect that comes when one shot is cut to another, known as *montage*.

Filmmakers have known from the beginnings of the art that one shot cut to another may yield a meaning contained in neither. The Russian director Sergei Eisenstein astonished the world in the 1920s with the power of such juxtaposition, and even the earliest pioneers of cinema knew that a shot of a heroine tied to the train track when intercut with a shot of a speeding locomotive would produce great emotion felt by the audience.

In theater, of course, such pictorial collisions were rarely if ever used. The basic unit of that medium is the scene. The scenes play differently each night because the audiences are different, and each night the actors learn to play the scenes according to the response of the audience that is engaging with them.

Whether the basic unit is the shot as in cinema, the event as in television, or the scene as in theater, one could say that basic unit is the emotional moment; how that moment is achieved differs in each.

It was clear in my first workshop at OCCC that even in Live Cinema, each shot had to be specific and capable of being cut against other shots; in other words, clear, specific shots were needed in order for the storytelling to go forward with cinematic syntax. Otherwise, the shots would merely be coverage of the components of play-like scenes, such as the close, medium, and long shots of characters used in televising a play. I wanted to achieve a cinema-like expression, which required that the shots not just be coverage, but real building blocks in the cinematic telling of the story.

Current live television usually involves a play or musical produced on a theatrical basis, with a defined set and if possible, one with a sense of unity, such as a courtroom drama, or a play in a definable setting, such as *12 Angry Men* or *On Golden Pond*. I realized that I had imagined my piece within the logic of some kind of scenic setting, but given the fact that I had only some basic furniture, props, and no real sets (see Chapter 5 on sets), I began to create shots for their own sake and diminished the logic of the sets. For example, I needed a shot in which the wife is in bed and the phone rings and the husband answers it, and tells his mother he'll be right over. The gymnastics to do this shot was in fact totally illogical in terms of where the husband and phone were relative to the bed and the awakened wife.

This simple adjustment told me that the set is not important, or is certainly secondary to the shot. That meant that what normally in television is covering the actors could now become something more powerful: shot creation. Whereas usually the director takes the camera and puts it where the actors are in the set, setting the camera on the scene, with the actor and set covered in it, now the set and actor would be manipulated within the camera frame to create the most compelling shot. The camera does not struggle to adapt itself to where the actor is placed in the set, but rather the actor and set are manipulated to create a shot within the camera's view. This implies that the scenic designer, rather than giving the scene a defined set as in live television, provides scenic elements that can be added to the actors within the shot. In effect this means that the *succession* of shots, much like the storyboard in the preparation of an animated film, is created with the actors themselves going from one shot to the next in performing the story.

Hitchcock knew this with his use of oversized props to enable his shot designs, but there are only a few instances in the history of cinema or television in which this is the method. In the mid-1940s, J. Arthur Rank studios in London briefly attempted a system of production known as Independent Frame, developed by David Rawnsley, in which the shot was pre-designed (much like a Disney storyboard) and the setting for each shot was erected on a rostrum that could be shot in mass-production style (using elements of rear projection). However, this system was created to reduce the time and money to make movies and not to enable live performance. Only a few movies were ever made on the system. I once tracked down Richard Attenborough, and asked if he remembered much about the Independent Frame film he had appeared in as a young actor. He told me that the actors felt very confined working in the pre-designed shots, and ultimately the system was abandoned, and yet the clever rostrums long remained a useful tool at Pinewood Studios.

WHAT GIVES LIVE TELEVISION ITS PARTICULAR LOOK?

When you watch a live television production, or for that matter any televised dramatic or musical show, whether it is recorded or live, you know immediately that it is television. Why? Certainly, when movies are shown on television they still look like movies, so it's not an issue of the transmission per se. The reasons are several. First, live TV tends to use multiple cameras that rely on big zoom (telephoto) lenses allowing the camera to frame both close and long shots without changing position and helping prevent one camera from seeing another. This is how coverage is achieved in television, whether for a soap opera or a live musical production. These large lenses have many layers of glass and require a lot of light, making a large overhead lighting grid essential. Not only do such grids provide enough light to enable these lenses to function, but they also satisfy an executive dictum that the scenes of the show be well and evenly illuminated.

Cinema lighting is very different, in that shots are done one at a time; a single camera can be placed close to the subject without fear of its being in front of other cameras. Often, flat (not zoom) lenses can be used, which are faster (much more sensitive to light), so over-illumination is not required, and the lighting can come from the floor rather than from an intense overhead grid. This means that a floor lamp or normal light appliances are sufficient to illuminate the scene; or light coming in from the windows or other floor-level lighting can be used, providing a beautiful balance of light and shadow, instead of the blasting light that an overhead lighting grid provides. It is this more cinematic lighting, along with the careful composition of shots, that gives the piece a cinematic look.

Certainly, not using zoom lenses presents other issues, since often these more normal cinema-type shots are in fact in the view of the other cameras; even if the cameras are well hidden, their shots are actually a compromise from those the director might prefer. This drawback was less apparent in the OCCC workshop because there were no actual sets, and it was relatively easy to hide a camera by putting it behind a plant or piece of furniture. But in the UCLA workshop, there were more formal sets, and although it was possible to hide the cameras, I found myself frustrated that I could not get the best shots, or at least the shots I wanted, because usually the camera would be smack in the middle of other important shots. This was definitely a limitation, although various solutions to this problem became apparent, and if there ever is a third workshop, I will employ some of these ideas to solve the problem.

In the UCLA workshop, I learned that I must find a method to enable fewer cameras to yield more shots. With this simple step, for example, reducing what were nine separate cameras to perhaps three, the job of placing them and hiding them from each other would of course be much easier. So, next time around I would have a number of 8K cameras, meaning cameras of more than four times the sharpness, resolution, and quality, and derive from one 8K master shot a number of closer shots. If I were to successfully hide one of these cameras, coming from a reverse angle, that angle opposite from where other cameras were aimed, electronically I could derive any number of closer shots, in addition to the primary master shot (the widest shot possible). So at my multiviewer (controls), I would see perhaps four individual closer shots all coming from that one hidden camera, and could choose at will which to use.

A few years ago, I watched *Amnesia*, a film by the fine director Barbet Schroeder that I quite enjoyed. It was shot in Ibiza, off the coast of Spain, and was about his mother. I thought it beautiful and effective, but was surprised when Barbet told me it had all been shot on an 8K camera, all in master shots, and that the various shots used for coverage—close-ups, two-shots, etc.—were all taken later from the master views. It reminded me of a book we studied in film school, *The Way of Chinese Painting*, in which it was demonstrated how a large painting could be broken up into many closer compositions that were very beautiful.

Essentially what Barbet was telling me was that all the shots in his film were recomposed out of a single high-resolution master shot, and thus were totally clear and in focus and acceptable as the shots of his film. What this would mean when one worked in Live Cinema is that rather than trying to hide seven or eight cameras in a scene, one could shoot one 8K master, or perhaps two or three 8K masters. This would mean far fewer cameras to hide, while during the performance, one could see the pre-conceived coverage or closer shots on the multiviewer, just as I was doing with nine cameras. I imagine that all the coverage from the perspective of one master might become boring or obvious (though I hadn't felt that way during *Amnesia*) and thus two masters would give your perspective variation. It doesn't answer how the camera in the reverse position could be made invisible other than by very cleverly hiding it in the set dressing or walls, or, as I did at UCLA, pre-shooting those difficult angles.

WHY EVEN TRY DOING LIVE CINEMA?

I must admit that during the workshops this question remained always present in my thoughts: Why even try doing this? Why give up the control the director has with classical cinema just for the sake of achieving the expressivity of live performance? If I achieved a truly cinematic look and result, and if my Live Cinema performance looked like a movie, then why didn't I just try to make this as a normal movie? What, in fact, does the live performance add? And how does the audience even know that the work is being performed live? Consider how you feel watching a televised baseball game, thinking it's really in the middle of the fifth inning and the score is tied, when you discover that, in fact, the game is over, and your team won. Immediately the game is like yesterday's newspaper: dead, flat, and unwatchable. What is the difference between knowing it is really live or prerecorded? Because the cinema, like theater before it, is only relevant in the experience it gives to an *audience*. What can the director do to make the live performance more apparent and enjoyable? In my second experimental workshop, all I was trying to do was to make the performance feel and behave just like a movie. Thus, I wasn't concerned about people accepting it as such, saying, "So what if it were live! It just seemed like a movie—I didn't even know it was live."

Several things occurred to me. First, the few mishaps and flaws in our second workshop performance were, in fact, telltale signs that this was a live performance, and thus some people actually felt the miscues were a blessing. This made me wonder if the director of Live Cinema should endeavor to put certain obstacles into it, so that during the performance the actors would intentionally be confronted by the fact that an essential prop had been left out, like a stepladder; or, perhaps, a direction given which in the moment would be near-impossible, or an actor in the moment of performance would discover a new obstruction he had to overcome. Perhaps that would give the show little crisis moments so that the audience would revel in the live nature of things (more on obstacles later).

Each of my two workshop broadcasts began with a black card explaining the nature of the production, but perhaps there should be moments beforehand, along with this statement, in which clips of various behind-the-scenes preparation are shown—the various settings, cameras, crew, and situation, drawing you into the expectation that this will be a live presentation. Just as with live baseball, much of your enjoyment is in your mind, your awareness that the performance in all its flaws is live. Perhaps if you see and know that everyone is getting ready for a live show, one in which no one yet knows the outcome, and your watch is synchronized with the actual time, then you'll feel it's live and thus be on pins and needles, wondering if it can all be pulled off and come together.

2

A SHORT HISTORY OF FILM
AND TELEVISION

While the Scottish-American inventor Alexander Graham Bell is known for his innovations in the transmission of sound, he was also interested in the possibility of using electricity to see things from a distance. Bell's telephone was actually intended to be an aid to deaf people trying to learn how to speak. He wanted the instrument also to transmit pictures, in order to help those who couldn't hear. The difficulties of electric pictures were more daunting than sound alone, and it is said the idea was abandoned. I own a copy of the June 4, 1908, issue of the British science journal *Nature*, where the idea of electric television is first formally mentioned, called at that time "Distant Electric Vision" by English scientist Shelford Bidwell in his article "Telegraphic Photography and Electric Vision."

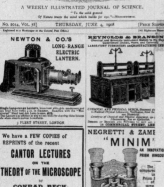

The problem of telegraphic photography is often associated in the popular mind with that of distant electric vision, or "seeing by electricity," as it has been called. According to a telegram from the Paris correspondent of the *Times,* dated April 28, the latter problem is now engaging the attention of M. Armengaud, president of the French Society of Aërial Navigation, who "firmly believes that within a year, as a consequence of the advance already made by his apparatus, we shall be watching one another across distances hundreds of miles apart." It may be doubted whether those who are bold enough to at-

solution upon the lines indicated, there is no reason beyond that of expense why vision should not be electrically extended over long distances.

The idea hardly belonged to Bell or Bidwell alone, but was being investigated by scientists of many countries, including Russia, France, and Japan. The mechanical basis of "distant electric vision" produced unsatisfactory and unclear images, but in a response to Bidwell's article, another scientist, the Scottish electrical engineer A. A. Campbell-Swinton, stated the problems could be solved by two beams of cathode rays. This is precisely what the great Russian scientist Boris Rosing was pursuing, aided by his student Vladimir Zworykin. Independently, in the 1920s, a fifteen-year-old American, Philo Farnsworth, sketched his plan for electronic television on the blackboard of his high school. He went on to develop and patent it, leading to a long and difficult conflict with RCA, who had hired Zworykin, and used the full force of their power to wrest the patent away from Farnsworth.

But in a quirk of progress, it was the motion picture that first came to the public. Inspired by British photographer Eadweard Muybridge's experiments with motion, "moving pictures" were made using a special camera called the Kinetograph by the American wizard Thomas Edison; the French Lumière brothers continued these advances by projecting such images on a large screen— giving birth to the cinema. Surprisingly, Edison's motion picture emerged in 1893, some years after mechanical television was introduced, so that when modern electronic television finally emerged in 1927, it had learned its visual language and artistic landscape from the film industry. What might have happened if television had appeared first? We will never know.

COMMERCIALS

Once RCA had introduced its new perfect form of "Distant Vision"— officially replaced by two words, *tele* and *vision*, one being Greek and the other Latin, Tele-Vision—it quickly assumed the enormous popularity that commercial radio had earlier enjoyed in the 1920s and 1930s. American television adopted the use of "commercials," which AT&T had fostered and which had proven so effective in radio. Even David Sarnoff, who was chairman of RCA and later NBC, was first skeptical and then surprised that the new medium would follow this model. He and other leaders around the world assumed that broadcasting, both radio and television, would be a cultural medium for their respective nations, but the draw of radio sponsorship by soap and breakfast cereal companies proved irresistible. Television slavishly followed the commercial precedent of radio, and programs were presented by sponsors in the United States—the only country in the world to do so.

Television remained impossible to record and edit beyond the crude method known as the Kinescope, in which a 16mm film camera was set up to photograph the cathode ray screen. The Kinescope yielded a poor quality, and was mainly used to enable time shifting between the time zones of the vast United States. Moreover, the flat-rate pricing charged by AT&T for the long-distance lines necessary to connect the country favored companies with many hours of programming, and forced pioneer networks such as the scrappy DuMont Television Network out of business. An actual television tape recorder wasn't developed until 1956—with cumbersome video editing systems soon to follow.

Film, on the other hand, could be shot, mulled over, and easily edited—and from this basis the early film directors pioneered many innovations that television was later to follow: the close-up, parallel editing, and montage. In the fertile days of silent cinema, artistry flourished. Producers were glad to have two 20-minute reels of anything they could show to the crowds rushing to the nickelodeons, putting filmmakers in a position to experiment. In Germany there emerged a concentration of great talent, which congregated at the UFA studios in Berlin and turned out masterpieces that will live forever. G. W. Pabst, Fritz Lang, F. W. Murnau, and Ernst Lubitsch, among many others, were exploring this new art form with passion and imagination. In fact, the work of telling a story through pictures was gaining such impressive ground that Murnau later said, "The talking picture represents a great step forward in the cinema. Unfortunately, it has come too soon; we had just begun to find our way with the silent film and were beginning to exploit all the possibilities of the camera. And now here are the talkies and the camera is forgotten while people rack their brains about how to use the microphone." Even the young Alfred Hitchcock was sent to make a film in Germany, where he wandered around the UFA studios, watching and noting well the extraordinary things going on, which he was to make effective use of throughout his long career.

The history of movies went quickly from the nickelodeon and simple two-reel features to beautiful works of art flowing from Berlin in the 1920s, then from major cities and eventually from Hollywood. Because television in its earliest form could not be recorded or edited, the purposes proposed for Distant Electric Vision were quite different from film, and very limited. It was thought to be useful for people to see and talk to a loved one far away, much like today's FaceTime, or for police to check a suspects lineup in a distant city, or perhaps to witness a political or sporting event. Television was greatly limited because of the quality of its picture, owing to its mechanical basis, but ultimately it was to emerge as an electronic medium due to the work of Boris Rosing, Vladimir Zworykin, and quite independently, high school student Philo Farnsworth.

In 1934, Farnsworth, financially stressed from his long legal battle with RCA, licensed his patents to Germany, enabling the emerging Nazi regime to later make use of television for propoganda during World War II. Great Britain, meanwhile, was still tied to the mechanical television of John Logie Baird, the Scottish innovator and engineer, who began broadcasting in 1927. There was a heartrending moment when Baird came face to face with Farnsworth's electronic screen, and saw for himself that his own system was antiquated and inferior. Thus the era of electronic television began, with the giant RCA, which had obtained the Zworykin patents and was fighting against Farnsworth—until they broke the young genius's spirit. As with so many histories of scientific development, the path was paved with tears.

THE FIRST GOLDEN AGE OF TELEVISION

Television in America began in earnest at the conclusion of World War II, just as many young GIs found themselves in New York, Chicago, and other major cities. Many who had participated in the artistic units in the army, touring theater efforts, and even the signal corps were anxious to find employment in the new industry. Those who came to New York found an especially fertile place to begin. The New York theater was also resplendent with fine actors who worked mostly in the evening, and so were available for rehearsal in the mornings and afternoons, and had Sundays free to shoot. A few studios were set up in the city, one famously at the top of Grand Central Station, another, DuMont's, at Wanamaker's department store at 9th Street and Broadway.

At first, good material was hard to come by. The powerful film industry, wary of this new form of entertainment, was resistant to any cooperation unless they were able to buy into or control the new art form. For forty or so years, the motion picture studios had been optioning and buying all the available literary materials—novels, histories, and plays, as well as all rights of their authors. Little was available to the talented young television producers, such as Fred Coe,* who had come from the Yale School of Drama, to put into production. At first they tried classics, public domain material such as Shakespeare, but such programming suffered in comparison to the high-quality and exciting material accumulated over the years by the competing film industry.

But a change of thinking arrived with the influx of postwar tal-

---

*I was fortunate to work with Fred Coe on the script of *This Property Is Condemned*, and over time I've come to realize that he was the pivotal figure behind the first Golden Age of Live Television.

ent. The new television directors, such as Arthur Penn, who had recently been discharged from the armed services, remembered that they knew young writers in the service with whom they had worked. Many in the new industry thought that they'd have nothing to lose by letting these recently discharged young playwrights try their hand, writing about anything they wanted to. The soon-to-be famous writers included the likes of Paddy Chayefsky, JP Miller, Gore Vidal, and Rod Serling, and their work, contemporary and intimate, was incendiary in this new medium. Thus began the Golden Age of Live Television. Sidney Lumet told me that when he was recruited from the theater to work on *Danger* for CBS, he encountered an exciting TV director, to whom he was assigned as an assistant, and his own assistant was an even younger man named John Frankenheimer. One day their boss, this first whiz director of television, told them, "Well boys, I'm going to audition for a new musical here on Broadway." That man was Yul Brynner, who would then land the starring role in *The King and I*, enabling Lumet to be promoted to director, and Frankenheimer to be stage manager.

The "live" period that ensued is duly memorialized as the Golden Age of Television. Extraordinary live productions such as *Marty, Days of Wine and Roses, Requiem for a Heavyweight, Patterns*, and *The Comedian* will be forever treasured as classics.

Of the directors of live television, John Frankenheimer tended toward a more cinematic style, as he aspired to be a film director. His live productions were in my mind the beginning of what I'd call Live Cinema, as they told their stories not only with the finest of acting and writing, but with exciting cinematic shots and editing. Although Frankenheimer wasn't chosen to direct the later film version of *Days of Wine and Roses*, his live television version with Cliff Robertson and Piper Laurie is to me far more moving and emotional, due to the immediacy and the heartbreaking reality that live performances gave the story, combined with Frankenheimer's cinematic vision.

I'll never forget one day in the mid-1950s when my mother came to my room to say that my father was on television. I ran down to the television in his studio two floors below, and there he was—playing the flute on our TV. But I turned around, and there he also was, sitting at his piano watching the broadcast. It was astounding. He explained that the program had been recorded on the new Ampex video recorder (with young Ray Dolby on the team) and it was absolutely impossible to know it wasn't live. The Ampex video recorder came out in 1956 (the year before Frankenheimer's *The Comedian* was broadcast), and was followed by Toshiba's video helical scan tape recorder in 1959, which solved the problem of tremendous bandwidth required by video by means of a rotating pickup head. For me, *The Comedian is* the masterpiece of Live Cinema because it was shot in a cinematic style, and everything it did, it did in a great live performance. The shows possessed a life and reality in their performances that made them memorable. Frankenheimer went on to do more major productions, both live and pre-recorded, some for *Playhouse 90*, such as *The Turn of the Screw*, starring Ingrid Bergman, and a two-part *For Whom the Bell Tolls*. But with the new video recorder, Hollywood finally caught up with television and economics prevailed as the Golden Age succumbed to edited film production and comedies such as *I Love Lucy* followed by decades of filmed entertainment.

A NEW ERA OF POSSIBILITIES

More than half a century has elapsed since the end of that exceptional creative period, and television has gone on into any number of areas. Today, sports remain the most popular programming available, and are "live" by necessity. The many awards shows that have slavishly come upon the heels of the Academy Awards are also live. Aside from the phenomenon of all-news stations, following Ted Turner's brilliant concept of using satellites to create the superstation CNN in Atlanta, and a few live spectacles such as musicals and plays, television entertainment is largely a canned medium.

Interestingly, from the technology that has emerged from sports—satellite feeds and instant replay servers, as well as from a variety of other technologies, which are being introduced monthly—there is a rich array of equipment that could, if desired, be turned to storytelling. The days when television represented a console in the home and film was seen in a movie theater seem to be over. Television and movies are now pretty much the same thing, as *The Sopranos* and *Breaking Bad* have shown. Cinema can now be from one minute long to one hundred hours, seen anywhere, in the home, the theater, the church or community center, and anywhere around the world, thanks to satellites and digital electronics.

MY MOST PROPHETIC AND EMBARRASSING MOMENT

My friend Bill Graham, the rock music promoter and actor, always wanted to go to the Academy Awards, so in 1979, when I was invited to be a presenter, I gave him one of my two premium tickets, while my family sat in less well-positioned seats in another area. We both were dressed in tuxedos, and Bill enjoyed the show very much. But I noticed that he had brought with him a bag of cookies which he kept munching on. Never someone who'd sit by idly while another was eating, I reached over to the bag and took one of the cookies and ate it. His face paled and he said, "No, not those." I had no idea what this reaction was about. Somewhat later, an assistant of the Academy came to the aisle near my seat, and indicated it was time for me to leave and go backstage, in preparation to play my part in the show. I was to be one of the presenters of the "Best Director" award, along with the actress Ali MacGraw. Michael Cimino, a very sweet and shy man, won for *The Deer Hunter*. I am still too embarrassed to watch a clip of this event, even after so many years. As I stood at the podium about to announce the winner, no doubt feeling weird after whatever was in that cookie, continuously scratching my beard, I blurted out to countless millions of viewers around the world a nugget of future Live Cinema when I said:

> I'd like to say that I think we are on the eve of something that is going to make the Industrial Revolution look like an out-of-town tryout. I'm talking about the communication revolution and I think it is coming very quickly. I see a communication revolution that is about movies and art and music and digital electronics and computers and satellites and above all, human talent. It is going to make things that the masters of the cinema, from whom we have inherited this business, wouldn't believe to be possible.

I will always remember the stunned expression on Ali MacGraw's face when I launched into that unprompted speech!

A SECOND GOLDEN AGE OF TELEVISION

The period of filmmaking in the 1970s and early 1980s is thought of as a breakthrough in personal expression, and in later years became an inspiration to the next generation of filmmakers who were weaned on *Raging Bull*, *The King of Comedy*, *Chinatown*, *Taxi Driver*, *The French Connection*, *Manhattan*, and some of my films. However, these new auteurs realized at the same time that Hollywood had latched the gate on such a permissive period, and the opportunity to make films in this tradition was over. So they turned to long-form cable television, resolved to make that kind of personal cinema. This led to a second Golden Age of Television, with such productions as *The Sopranos*, *Breaking Bad*, *The Wire*, *Mad Men*, and *Deadwood*, to list just a few. In addition, throughout this entire period, starting in 1975, there was live TV bordering on Live Cinema in the form of *Saturday Night Live* (*SNL*).

SATURDAY NIGHT LIVE

SNL has managed to be both popular and relevant—no doubt popular because it is relevant. It is performed live, and it comes close to being Live Cinema because it often tells a story in a sequence of shots rather than in the simple coverage of a stage event. This is not new; Ernie Kovacs often did this, as did Sid Caesar, Imogene Coca, and Jackie Gleason. The original *Honeymooners* comedy show often parodied current events. Certainly these shows are as enjoyable as recorded shows as they are live ones, attested to by the valuable archival versions. (Some of *SNL* has always made use of recorded portions, even filmed parts, and EVS replay servers.) What, then, is the difference between those two ways of seeing the show? *SNL* is "live" in essence, because that fact enables it to be immediately relevant to current and topical events. *SNL's* parody of breaking news is able to incorporate facets of politics that have just occurred. This is the essence of live events: simply put, you don't know what will happen until it happens.

So *SNL* is by its very definition a Live Cinema show, just as any sporting event or coverage of a news event must be, whether it's seen and enjoyed later or not. The popular comedy show is a parody of current affairs and thus must wait for those affairs to show themselves before it can make fun of them. It's better to view them in the freshness of the moment, but there's also a second mode, when you see them later. It's a little like a family photograph, which is enjoyed immediately on the first look, but also sometimes even more so later on when the passage of time has made it "vintage."

Recently, I saw Woody Harrelson's *Lost in London*, shot with a single camera in one night, and broadcast live to 500 theaters. It was, in my opinion, a total success—funny, full of energy, and an amazing display of imaginative technology. It of course got through the "live" issue by being a one-shot film, like *Russian Ark*, *Birdman*, and *Victoria*. I believe it may have been the first Live Cinema event sent directly to theaters, but perhaps that distinction belongs to the magnificent Andrea Andermann production of *La Traviata*. Harrelson's "one camera" decision covered imaginative staging without switching cameras, following the impressive acting tour de force of Harrelson and his cast by dragging the audience along on the romp. It proved that if a project is well-rehearsed, the actors are up to the challenge, as this cast certainly was. *Lost in London* is certainly a milestone in the history of Live Cinema.

THE VALUE OF PERFORMANCE

The tradition of the virtuoso conductor was born in the nineteenth century. Often these artists were attached to the opera house of a particular city, among them Dresden and Berlin, with the benefit of a nobleman's patronage. Some, such as Richard Wagner, Hans von

Bulow, Richard Strauss, and Gustav Mahler, were composers, while others were not. Either way, they remain the closest equivalent to the contemporary film director, given their power over the production and supervision of everything connected with it: decor, staging, chorus and dance, costumes, and of course the acoustics and music. The costly and complex opera productions were something at the level achieved in modern filmmaking, with one major difference: on the night of the first showing, the conductor stood up before the audience, raised his baton, and with its downbeat a live performance began. Often it was something the audience would not forget their entire life. Imagine being present at the first performance of Verdi's *La Traviata*, the story of a young man who loses himself in his love for a courtesan, or Wagner's epic music-drama *Tristan und Isolde*— or for that matter, imagine if you had been there when Tennessee Williams's great stage dramas *A Streetcar Named Desire* or *The Glass Menagerie* were first performed, or *West Side Story*, or any first performance of any great classic. Even a great initial failure, like the premiere of Bizet's seductive opera *Carmen* or Debussy's symbolist *Pelléas et Mélisande*, was memorable. Is that long-held concept of performance worth hanging onto, even when we have evolved to a time where most of our experience of art is canned? All of cinema, most of television, and our enjoyment of music and pictures are now based on recordings.

HOW IMPORTANT IS PERFORMANCE?

As we have seen, the most popular live aspect of television is live performance, and the most popular live television performance is sports. Many traditional forms of live performance are increasingly out of reach of audiences. The theater and opera have more and more become localized, particularly in New York, with ticket prices at prohibitively high levels. Besides, the offerings are rarely contemporary works, but usually old ones with the addition, if you are lucky, of movie stars appearing in limited runs. Rock shows are performed in an arena with tens of thousands of spectators and with very high ticket prices; most likely you are so far from the stage that despite it being a live event, it feels distant and automated, and the live part is hard to get at.

In reflection, I find it very interesting that at the beginning of the 1900s, many serious thinkers and writers were pondering the "future of the theater," with only scant mention of cinema, which was what the future of the theater was to be. In 1919, George Pierce Baker, a professor of playwriting at Harvard and later the founder of the great graduate program of theater at Yale, hinted marginally:

> Today the motion picture show has driven mere melodrama from our theatres, yet who will deny that the "movie" in its present form subordinates everything to action? Even the most ambitious specimens, such as *Cabiria* and *The Birth of a Nation*, finding their audiences restless under frequent use of the explanatory "titles" which make clear what cannot be clearly shown in action, hasten to depict some man hunt, some daring leap from a high cliff into the sea, or a wild onrush of galloping white-clad figures of the Ku Klux Klan.

And Eugene O'Neill, Baker's student at Harvard, who sought the future American theater in many theatrical techniques from the past, admitted that "a stage play combined with a screen talky background could make alive visually and vocally the memories, etc. in the minds of the characters." This was a concept he would abandon, but return to with his 1942 one-act tour de force *Hughie*. "Talkies,"

O'Neill believed, had the potential to be "a medium for real artists if they got a chance at it."

Curious, I went through book after book, among them Kenneth Macgowan's *The Theatre of Tomorrow*, William Archer's *Play-Making*, and Edward Gordon Craig's *On the Art of the Theatre*, and realized that the authors worried about the loss of traditional theatrical methods, such as the prologue, the soliloquy, asides, and masks, chorus, epilogue, and mute show. But the truth was that the theater wasn't going to move more to its past, it was going to move closer to something that for many years was staring it right in the face: the movies! Wherever you may go to experience a modern theatrical production, whether it be London's West End, New York's Broadway, or Germany's Bayreuth Festival, you can't escape the productions' attempt to be cinematic, to use projections to somehow attain the effect of the "close shot" or "weird angle," of the universe, or to borrow, as best as they can, the cinematic lexicon. I look at this attempt as theater trying to be movies, and then wonder if I am so crazy to want movies to take back the performance element of theater.

3

THE ACTORS, ACTING,
AND REHEARSAL

In the experimental workshops, I noted to myself emphatically that "the actors are the least of the problem." Yet in the film business, it is often the actors, especially the stars, who become the focus of the production's problems. You'll hear that they don't know their lines or are difficult, late, and critical of the script or production realities. Much of this is because actors, and indeed the stars, tend to be lovers of acting and cinema, and are the best bet of all movie-making personnel to become directors themselves: Charlie Chaplin, Buster Keaton, Charles Laughton, Laurence Olivier, Ida Lupino, among an endless list of others.* Thus their criticism and insights about the way the film is going, or about the script, are often justi-

---

*More actors became directors than from any other category of movie profes-sionals, including writers, editors, and photographers.

fied. When first considering a format where actors must be able to know the entire script by memory, people (oddly) will ask, will the actors be able to do it? Of course we all know that traditionally the cast of a theater production does just this, and it is expected of them. It all comes down to the rehearsal, which, regrettably, often isn't a part of the movie production.

Let me explain how my workshops went. Both had rehearsals which lasted about a week. These were not unlike rehearsal periods in the theater, with read-throughs, stumble-throughs, run-throughs, and dress rehearsals. Once inside the rehearsal or Actors Room, as I call it, one rule is paramount: the cast must always be in character. (Another is "Abandon fear, all ye who enter.") The actors must use the characters' names while addressing each other, and I do the same. They cannot say things like "My character just loves ice cream," but rather, "I love ice cream." Surprisingly, being someone other than yourself through an eight-hour day is exhausting, and some slip out of it, reverting to discussing their character in the third person, but that is strictly discouraged. The rehearsal period is a workout, and like any exercise it is eventually rewarded with a developing sense of the character that is being played.

For me, rehearsal is composed of a variety of exercises, improvisations, games, and staging efforts, and I have endeavored to make use of the same basic rehearsal process throughout my filmmaking career. I feel it's important that the day's work is a pleasure, and I always vary the activities so they're never boring and provide a real active workout—in character building. The rehearsal room contains a set of rehearsal furniture: lightweight chairs of a single type, and card tables. They are easily dragged about, and form endless combinations to make up all rehearsal possibilities. Two or three chairs can be a couch, four chairs a car, two tables can be a dining table, and combinations of these basic elements can be imagined to be anything needed to stage the scenes. Along one wall I always have one or two banquet tables covered with hand props: a telephone, some plastic cups and dishes, a camera, a cane, and so on. And near to the rehearsal prop table is a rack with hats of many types, and a few pieces of wardrobe: a shawl, a boa, and a few jackets. Other than the rehearsal furniture, the prop tables, and the rack of clothing, there is nothing in the room aside from the assembled cast.

The first day of my rehearsals usually has two read-throughs of the script. The first is a read-through without stopping, just to get a sense of the text. The second one, usually after lunch, is stop and go, with anyone able to make a point or ask a question, and the director has the opportunity to clarify, to help with intention or with pronunciation, or for any other reason. In the course of the read-throughs, the director tries to make clear that the rehearsal room is a place of safety, where no one need fear doing something wrong, or doing badly; the point is made that this is a place of play and enjoyment. To make this clear, on that first day, we often engage in a few theater games or other "concentration" exercises. These games, which I'll talk about more later in the chapter, were devised and introduced by Viola Spolin in her book *Theater Games for Rehearsal* and taught by her son Paul Sills, and are fun to do, while also helping develop the actor's concentration and understanding of the natural hierarchy present in most relationships. It's important that the actors leave their first day of rehearsal having enjoyed themselves, and feeling safe and wanted.

Actors are also encouraged to wander over to the hat rack and prop table to take anything that catches their eye. The director should realize that the actors may be terrified at finally approaching work, and anything they can hold in their hands or put on their head may give them a degree of confidence. I've learned that no matter what problem you are having with an actor—chronic lateness, not knowing lines, an attack on the script, nastiness—most of those things come from the fact that they are afraid. As you alleviate their fears with whatever method, gradually the problems go away. Actors are asked to do a very difficult thing: to perform artistically with themselves as their instrument. It is a terrifying process.

On the days of rehearsal, the actor is led through various activities, rotating between improv, theater games, and attempts at the text, using the tables and chairs as a set and staging some of the scenes. You must vary these activities, so that the day is never boring. I don't place an emphasis on reading and working with the text. For one thing, one wants it to have a certain freshness, and repetition of the scenes will dim that. On the other hand, improvs, especially when designed to bring out certain characteristics of the roles or provide memories for the characters, are particularly helpful. I always do an improv between characters who have a relationship, either married, or in the same family, or work colleagues, by setting up with each actor privately an intention, and then a situation where they meet for the first time. In life, married couples remember details of how they met, the first time they broke up, how they got back together. Yet we expect our cast to play a married couple with none of these memories. So I try to provide them via improvisations.

IMPROVISATION DURING REHEARSAL

One of the biggest benefits that comes from extensive improv during rehearsal is that it gives an opportunity to examine the character and practice situations of the text without exhausting the freshness of the dialogue. This is of great importance. Often fine actors, including Marlon Brando, try to not know the lines or rehearse them often, so that during filming, the performance is lifelike, in that the character is saying the dialogue for the first time. Marlon, working on *The Godfather* and *Apocalypse Now*, was fond of saying, "You can't care, or they'll see it on your face." For my purposes, improvisation offers a way to find new meaning in the character's situations and problems without reciting lines. Also, it allows you to develop aspects of a relationship you feel are missing, such as the inherent love between siblings, who grew up and played together, even though as adults they are enemies or have some bitter feelings. Improvisation can provide a history with another character, to make a "deposit in the emotional bank account" of a relationship. When the scene requires that the husband tell his wife that he loves another woman, it is worthwhile that he also has that memory of their first meeting, or first breakup, or the joy of the first child. Every decisive moment between people is fraught with many memories. As the actors don't have those memories to call upon, improvisation can establish them. Of course it's not as if the character literally recalls all of the possible memories, but they are there—just as they are there in real life, to be flashed on or not, to emerge or not in a natural way.

When setting up an improv, it's a good idea to tell the participants in private (in their ear, so to speak), what their real intention is. To one: "You want to borrow $5,000 from her." To the other person, something likely to cause some conflict or complication to be worked out in the scene: "He's owed you $4,000 for years and never mentions it." Also, as their rehearsal set is usually only some chairs and tables, it's a good idea to make things as specific as possible: "This is at the cafeteria at school, and the only chair is next to her." The director should be nimble in coming up with ideas; often the best ones are suggested by a need to set a characteristic or tendency you'd like to discover in the character. So a fresh and interesting improv idea must be produced instantly, with a specific setting and an intention for each participant. Everything must be specific—and designed to work the characters to a full extent. Day after day of such improv is likely to thicken the sauce you are making, while also turning work into play. Also, any sensual elements that you introduce into the situation—actual food, music or dancing, touching—all intensify the improv and make it stick, so that it is available during the performance period.

The first rehearsal of *The Godfather* in 1971 was in a back room of the legendary Patsy's, a restaurant in New York. It was to be the first time the cast members would meet Marlon Brando, and of course they were all excited and frightened at this prospect, as I was as well. I arranged a table like one at home, and sat Marlon at its head, Al Pacino to the right and James Caan to the left, John Cazale to Al's right, and Bobby Duvall to Jimmy's left. I asked my sister Talia to serve the food to them, and they ate dinner together. When the meal was finished, that family existed for the first time, and those relationships learned during it remained throughout the difficulties of shooting the film. That's when I first realized that food was a binding element and made the improv persist for a long time. In subsequent rehearsals, especially large group improvs, which can go on for several hours, and in which the various characters visit one another in their homes and work out various suggested intentions, I found that actually preparing and handling food, for example taking cold cuts out of the wrapping, preparing sandwiches, and then eating them, had the effect of allowing a sense-memory to be invoked in the other aspects of the improv, as did touching, and dancing to music.

One of the best improvs I ever did was in 2008 during the filming of *Tetro* in Buenos Aires, when I asked the entire cast to come to a costume party, in a costume chosen not by themselves as the actor, but by the character they were playing. At this party there was a buffet of food, and a band. Things evolved during those few hours that were extremely valuable to the process of transformation, and one by one, each actor turned into his or her character. Actually, it was during that session when I first realized that the actors do not turn into the characters—in fact, the characters turn into the actors. This might be saying the same thing, but as the actor is flesh and blood, and the character is a spirit-like phenomenon, the process is more correctly understood as the effort that leads to the eventual inhabitation of the actor by the character.

I recall a great story Gene Hackman once told me about his first few weeks of *The French Connection*. He had no idea who his character was. He wore a funny hat, he tried various things, but the character just wouldn't come. Then one cold morning, he went to the craft services table, picked up a doughnut and dunked it into his hot coffee, took a single bite, and threw the doughnut away. "That's him," came a voice from behind him. It was Billy Friedkin, the director, who was always watching. Gene said after that, he had his character.

On the day when the cast is to leave the Actors Room for the stage or studio where the shooting will take place, I always work late, stalling lunch. The actors begin to get antsy as they are growing hungry, and then late in the day, perhaps even at 3:00 PM, and without our having had lunch, I lead them to the stage, where their chairs and tables have been set up, and instruct them on what will be a large, long group improv, giving each actor an intention, and designating areas to be so-and-so's house or room.

But then I point to several large grocery bags filled with cold cuts and rolls, drinks, etc. and explain that they are to perform the improv while preparing lunch and eating together. There's usually great relief when they realize they're going to eat, and they go to their various tasks in character-building agreeably, while dividing the food prep tasks according to their character, and talk, interact, and eat together. What they experience now in the space they will work in is never forgotten—and they make the transition from the rehearsal room to the shooting stage with pleasure, cemented to the enjoyment of preparing and eating the food together.

THEATER GAMES

These games, devised by Viola Spolin, whose book I've cited, are for the most part concentration exercises and hierarchical situations and games. Most importantly, they are fun and a relief to the actors, who, whether they know it or not, are struggling to spend a day wherein they must remain in character. The concentration exercises also build a focus of attention when played each day, and develop the ability to sense what your colleagues are about to do or say, something that is enormously valuable when a dramatic or comedy situation is being played.

Sound Ball is an easy starter. The group stands in a circle and I speak while bouncing an imaginary ball. I explain that I will toss this ball to someone, who must catch it and then throw it to someone else in the circle. But I make a sound when I throw it, and the person who catches it must repeat the sound, and then throw it to someone else while making their own sound. After a few tries they get it, and can rapidly catch and re-throw the make-believe ball, making the proper sounds as they do. At that point I introduce a second imaginary ball, and now they are keenly focused as they catch and throw two balls, with the appropriate sounds. Then I add a third ball. After a while they become quite skillful; at the same time, they are being united by the game and enjoying becoming a skillful group. This game can go on and on; in one variant, the sounds must follow the alphabet, and with the second ball, the alphabet in reverse. The game is difficult at that point, but a practiced group of actors can do it, and they also can do the many other tasks that will be given them where concentration is all-important.

A hierarchical game implies that in most human situations there's always a boss and a chain of sub-bosses and their assistants. People, especially children, have a sixth sense as to who has the power, and respond differently to that person and according to their own place in the lineup. One such game is Pick Up My Hat. A line is made, with each participant wearing a hat selected from the clothes rack. The first in the line is the boss; in one of many scenarios, he or she is waiting at the ticket booth to get the reserved tickets to something. The ticket seller is instructed to be uncooperative, and eventually the boss gets angry and throws her hat to the ground, shouting to her assistant (next in line) to "pick up my hat." The assistant throws his hat in anger, saying the same thing to the next in line, and then picks up his boss's hat and puts it back on his head. Of course, the process runs through the entire line. (I have a theory I hold as to why people in their cars in traffic behave so ridiculously. It is that in such a setting, encased by steel and glass, each person feels that for once, they are not stuck in a hierarchy and can behave as they want.)

I always divide the text, no matter how short, into three acts, and during the rehearsal period, alongside the many theater games and improvs and other hijinks thought up in the moment, we begin staging the actual scenes using our multipurpose chairs and tables as well as a few hand props and clothing articles. Soon, we are able to do a run-through, without interruption, of the first act, and then the other acts, until as the rehearsal period is coming to an end, before the big food improv which helps us leave our safe Actors Room, we can do a run-through of all three acts. By then, quite automatically, the cast know their lines and are able to perform as a whole the entire piece.

It is because of these methods that the actors are never a problem during the subsequent steps of Live Cinema. They have been prepared and encouraged as a group, have been worked and exercised through many aspects of their characters, and are capable of performing the entire piece without their scripts. Certainly, this is not different from the rehearsal period of a theater production, but quite different from ninety-nine percent of film preparation, where if there is any rehearsal time, it tends to be used bussing the actors to the intended locations and trying to get a leg up on the ultimate staging and shooting of the film shots. There are a million variations of these theater games and the actors love playing them. I find them a useful way to make clear that the process of our rehearsal together is nothing to fear and, in fact, we are playing together; our work together is difficult and daunting, but nevertheless enjoyable play and fun.

Just as water is composed of hydrogen and oxygen, and salt of sodium and chlorine, it has always been my contention that cinema is made up in equal parts of two essential ingredients, acting and writing. Needless to say, these are the two aspects that are examined, developed, and perfected during the time in the rehearsal room. There is little more than acting and writing at hand here, and the focus is on those primal elements.

4

EQUIPMENT AND TECHNICAL SPECIFICATIONS

I n this chapter dealing with equipment and technical specifics I borrow the format from the beloved ASC cinematographer's manual.

THE CAMERAS

Whereas cinema digital cameras are 24p (23.98 progressive frames per second), the standard in television in the United States is 60i (59.94 interlaced fields per second). Much equipment intended for sports and other broadcasting is thus at a frame rate different from cinema. Shooting at 24 frames per second has a cinematic quality that is already familiar to movie audiences, something I feel is important to try to strive for with Live Cinema. In Oklahoma, our NewTek TriCaster was compatible with 24p signals, so we were able to set all of the cameras to 24p. At UCLA, we again set each of our 40 digital cameras to 24p mode:

Canon EOS C300
Sony PXW-FS5 and PXW-FS7
Blackmagic Studio
Blackmagic Micro Studio

To bridge the gap between our cinema cameras (each set to 24p mode) and our EVS/broadcast environment (60i) we converted each camera signal from 24p to 60i using 40 Blackmagic Teranex Express frame rate converters, one computer per camera.

THE LENSES

Nothing has more influence over the beauty and quality of photography than the lens. Some of our cameras, such as the Blackmagic, allowed the use of adapters that would enable us to use C-mount for lenses; this meant that at UCLA we could use a treasury of old Bolex 16mm flat (prime) lenses that the school had on hand. These gave a particular vintage cinematic look, as well as greater speed and a quality that was pleasingly soft around the edges and not overly sharp and crisp like modern lenses.

THE MIXING BOARD

Our video mixing board was an early production EVS DYVI switcher. This was a new board which was given its first big job on our UCLA project. One of the original developers and lead software designers came from Germany to help configure it, to write custom code and create new features, and to make sure that it could do what we were asking of it. The DYVI switcher is essentially a computer that is emulating a standard video mixer, giving us tremendous ability to program it to our needs. With 40 cameras, 14 video streams from three EVS XT3 replay servers, and two additional streams from nonlinear editing systems, we had numerous individual preview streams (imagine 66 thumbnail images populating the video monitor wall) to keep track of.

The DYVI can be programmed to be set up in a "story mode," where each scene could be configured and saved as its own stage. That meant we could configure the multiviewer settings for each stage to display particular camera and replay server outputs on the multiviewer monitors. Because our custom DYVI configuration used two multiviewer outputs, we could have the custom display for the current stage on one multiview monitor and the next custom display for the next stage on the other multiview monitor. With clever programming from our German developer, the active monitor's background could be colored red and the preview multiview background grey. When we'd go to scene 2, the background color of the multiview for that stage would turn red, and the other multiview monitor would be programmed by our technical director to display the pertinent cameras and server streams for scene 3 (the next stage) with a grey background. All of this equipment is available for rental or purchase.

In the mid-1990s, sound mixing boards developed into in the form of computer-based interfaces and control surfaces from such companies as Digidesign. The dedicated sound mixing board, expensive and with only one purpose, was replaced by this newer form, a computer taught to emulate a mixing board, with a surface of assignable sliders and equalization buttons already familiar to sound mixers. All industry standard TV switchers have been digital for some time, but they are hardware-based, while the DYVI is software-based. This gives it extreme programmability, which at my second experimental workshop we tested to the fullest. The system's principal programmer and creator of the DYVI board, Jürgen Obstfelder, spent some days with us, teaching our technical director Teri Rozic the operational aspects of the DYVI and then two weeks working with her to develop new software code for our purposes. Teri told me our project would not have been possible with the software currently used in mixing boards, the standard of the industry. Some industry-standard switchers do have programmable multiviewer outputs, but they do not currently have the elaborately customizable multiviewer abilities we utilized. Having a video mixing board that could be reprogrammed to the specific needs of Live Cinema was in my opinion a must, despite the fact that this meant all was relying on a new mixing panel that had never been used before.

Some of the configurations we used enabled the relevant live camera and replay signals or feeds to be shown to the director according to what scene they were relevant to, changing instantly as each scene was approached. The many other tasks of the technical director, such as handling chroma key and input/output routing, were all organized on the board with a facility and speed not possible on a standard board.

Our collaboration with Jürgen and EVS made me wonder if, in fact, a system could be created that represented one or two steps before the moment of actual performance, which might further simplify the entire process. It would essentially be a program devised to support the entire Live Cinema process even at the script and storyboard phases.

I began to think of approaching this company with creating a device that would work seamlessly with the new DYVI board. One of its features would be that it could integrate the text of the script in sync with the timeline of the editing in such a way as to facilitate the process of editing image and sound during rehersal by moving around the text in word processing format. An editorial assistant would align the text along with dialogue and action and a musical time signature, a task something like syncing the dailies in early cinema. Once this task was accomplished, moving a block of text to some other location in the script or eliminating it would immediately determine where the image and sound, or one or the other, were placed in the editor's timeline. The rhythmic timeline would follow along much as in a musical score, so that the precision of the rhythmic measure, bar, and beat would allow the text to exactly determine the order and duration of the edited program, enabling all the elements to be synchronized (whether edited or not).

5

SCENERY AND LOCATION

I t is my belief that the style, mode, or classification of any motion picture could be re-approached as Live Cinema. When I heard that NBC had announced a live television production of *A Few Good Men*, I thought to myself, sure, that's a court martial story, with all the unity of the courtroom drama, perfect to be produced as a play and then covered with a television camera mentality (use of zoom lenses to cover the necessary shots) and the use of an extensive overhead grid to light it. This was similar to what was done on a live production of *On Golden Pond*, where an elaborate standing set, play-like staging, and classic conventional camera coverage made it resemble a typical television production. If I could choose any project I wanted for Live Cinema, I'd go to something nearly impossible to do as a live TV play, perhaps *Lawrence of Arabia* or something of similar grandeur. Obviously that tremendous film would push Live Cinema to its very limit (assuming it was even possible). But no matter how grand, you need to start the same way, by planning a storyboard of the shots you intend to get—and then figure out how to get them.

Now of course, there is a trick card in such speculation. Clearly one doesn't expect some Bedouin camel-handler to be standing throughout the production, ear to walkie-talkie, waiting for the command, "Send the camels!" The shots of camels may already have been recorded and loaded into the EVS machine, cued and ready to go. That fuels the contention that Live Cinema isn't really entirely live, and in truth, it isn't. Live Cinema, as it turns out, is a juggling act of many, many discrete pieces derived from live cameras and EVS-based cameras—which behave as if they are live but in fact can be juggled and used later, either fractions of a second later, or whenever wished. Then there is what is called in television sports "the package," a collection of EVS clips, often edited together quickly during a game and available to the director. This offers the possibility of having a pre-cut sequence available to add to the on-line live program.

Is this cheating? For me, it's about what percentage of the resultant production is truly live and what is not. The recent production of *Grease Live!*, the most exuberant of the recent live musicals and based more on the movie *Grease* than on the play *Grease*, was time-shifted so we in California saw a *recording* of a live broadcast of the show from New York. In truth, the original live broadcast lost sound for several minutes and flirted with rain, but this was actually corrected when it was shown on the West Coast three hours later. To me, pre-recorded (EVS) shots and sequences are part of Live Cinema, just as staged shots are part of the classic documentary film.

There has never been a documentary film, going back to the great classics such as Robert J. Flaherty's *Nanook of the North* (1922) that doesn't include any number of staged shots combined with reportage footage. When Flaherty was creating his evocative poem of the real lives of indigenous Inuit people, I am sure he told Nanook, "Go over to the fishing hole in the ice and catch a fish, which we'll put on the hook." All art cheats. As Flaherty said, "Sometimes you have to lie. One often has to distort a thing to catch its true spirit." Having some staged shots doesn't make something less than a great documentary. And having some EVS shots doesn't make a live baseball game any less live, and by the same token doesn't make a live performance of cinema less of a work of art. It is part of the recipe that a percentage of the production can be derived from other sources, other channels, and other methods.

My impression from working on two Live Cinema workshops was that it was like juggling a few hundred oranges in the air, and having them fall into place by virtue of skill, planning, luck, and magic. Cinema is by nature a complex collection of many images and sounds coming together to create emotional and intellectual impact. Whether those pieces are assembled over months or years of editing, as with a normal motion picture, or snatched out of the air on the fly, as in Live Cinema, the artistry and effect on audiences is determined by how beautiful its makers are able to perform. Having made it clear that by my definition, Live Cinema is made up of a percentage of true live camera feeds and a basket of pre-recorded, pre-edited components made available to live-switch during the performance, I'd like to move on to the issue of scenery and locations.

CREATING SHOTS

Shot creation involves the question of how one handles scenery, and the extent to which scenes or images are pre-recorded on location. After the cast has been suitably rehearsed and prepared according to the methods previously discussed, there comes the time when one must create the shots. Sure, if desired, one could work with a storyboard artist or team of storyboard artists, in a process which I named "pre-visualization" in the early 1980s when we were preparing *One from the Heart*. (The term met with resistance—"How can you have pre-visualization, shouldn't it be just called visualization?") I had no idea the phrase was still in use until many years later, when, during a tour of Pixar, I was asked, "Would you like to see the pre-visualization room?" I felt vindicated. Storyboarding is an expensive process, and Pixar and the other successful makers of 3-D animated films spend years creating, editing, reconceiving, and refining the storyboards of their films. Said simply, the storyboard in the pre-visualization process is the plan of the succession of shots that tell the story and specify the scenes.

One way of looking at Live Cinema is that you would have each frame (from the storyboard) standing on the set, while the actors rush from one to the next performing the scenes. And that is not far off from what actually happens. In the animation process of storyboarding, one doesn't really create the set and then cover the actors within as dictated by the logic of the set; rather, one starts making the desired shots, freely using the logic of the set to fit the needs of the shot.

In the Oklahoma experimental workshop I wanted to focus on the question of lighting, and so I decided basically not to have sets. Sets are expensive, and sets for cinema need great detail. The little money I had would be better spent on first trying to understand the creation of shots without the need of sets, so I could focus on the lighting.

I arranged some set pieces—a door, a window, along with set dressing and furniture, and basically let the set be only an occasional black curtain or scrim or just plain space. At first I thought the production would look something like Lars von Trier's 2003 film *Dogville*, in which an entire town is represented by a ground plan and furniture, to an eerie effect. I discovered, however, that even though like *Dogville* my set had no walls, the result looked very different. This was because of the lighting. *Dogville* is deliberately lit to reveal the lack of walls as a desired element, whereas our workshop used lighting to allow areas without walls to go black.

I resolved to light from the floor, with only some wrapped soft lights (snoots) from the grid: 50% of the lighting was from the grid, 40% film lights and projections from the floor, and 10% practicals (set lamps and other lighting fixtures). We bought a dozen or so LED movie lights, which could be rolled around easily, each powered by a battery left over from previous productions. These lights, along with the actual set dressings of table and floor lamps, and the several downward-focused soft light snoots, provided a cinema-style look. The new LED lights were moved around easily from scene to scene according to marks on the floor, because they had no trailing power cables.

The fact that we were using fast flat lenses rather than long TV-style zoom lenses meant that the exposure level was low and the mood and lighting tone were quite beautiful, with plenty of contrast and even some black—something television executives never allow. In truth, much of the look in television comes from the fact that edicts from the head office disallow anything but very bright, overall illumination, and mainly close shots, which is just the opposite of the approach taken in cinema. If I were to become the director of a soap opera and given some authority, I would be able to create a more cinematic look merely by switching off half of the lights. But this isn't permitted by the executives. Also, in the routine cutting pattern of the typical soap opera scene, one immediately goes from the establishing shot to the close-ups. In 2015, I spent some time attending rehearsals and tapings of various shows at CBS Television City including *The Young and the Restless, Dancing with the Stars,* and *The Late Late Show,* as well as live NFL football broadcasts. Once when I visited a soap opera taping, I suggested remaining on the master shot for an entire scene for the reason that the next scene would involve the close-ups, but was told that wouldn't be permitted because it was not the style of the show. Interestingly, the male prison population are among the biggest fans of long-running soaps like *The Young and the Restless,* and they prefer to see things uniformly lit, with plenty of close-ups and ladies in nice hairdos. Should anything vary from that formula, the fans would be greatly disappointed.

What I learned during the Oklahoma experiment was that with a variety of lighting, the shots took on a reality that resulted in a show that did not look like the great see-through vision of *Dogville,* but rather, had a different style of more discrete cinematic shots, where with so few elements—a mattress, a dining table, a door and little more—the audience was not aware so terribly much that in fact there were no sets.

SECOND PROOF-OF-CONCEPT WORKSHOP

When I was planning the second experiment at UCLA, I listed some questions I wanted to be able to answer. In particular, what would happen if I did have sets, but I was constrained by budget, since scenic settings are expensive? Here are some essential things that would be needed:

- *Modular sets.* Have some sort of modular set elements that could easily be dragged into place as needed to create the shots.
- *Electronic image screens.* Use LED or other electronic image screens to slide in and out to conjure scene elements into the sets that had been predesigned, photographed, or drawn. This would be a modern equivalent of the Translight screen used in movies: essentially, a large transparent photograph that can be integrated into a set to provide a view out a window, etc.
- *Digital settings.* Just as in big action films such as *Star Wars*, sets could be constructed within the computer, and then integrated live with the actors on the stage using green screen chroma key technology. This process generally requires that the camera shooting the scene be stationary. However, if it does move, or, to the extreme, if it is handheld (a style popular in contemporary cinema), it requires an elaborate electronic motion-control system. This works by triangulating the camera, locking it in to several points in the ceiling or walls, so that when the camera moves, the image on the green screen moves with it. This is tricky and costly, and so in the workshops I avoided it merely by not moving the camera when using green screen. But where budgets aren't so restrictive, it would be possible to use computer-generated scenics and yet move the camera freely with this method.

I decided not to use electronic (LED) screens as the new more modern form of a Translight, for cost reasons, but would love to explore that further in the future. For one thing, using that type of screen rather than green screen allows the camera freedom to move extensively, and even to be handheld. The cost of LED screens is coming down quickly, as you've noticed with your own home flat screen television, and now new technologies such as LG's OLED are becoming available, and display images that are wonderfully beautiful, with true blacks and vivid colors.

In creating a modular set at the UCLA workshop, I was inspired by the work of Edward Gordon Craig, a theater visionary from the early twentieth century. He was the son of the acclaimed British actress Ellen Terry. Craig was at first an actor himself, but eventually became the premier innovative scenic designer of the times. In the migration from realistic settings, he and other great artists, such as Adolphe Appia (wizard of stage lighting and décor), imagined more abstract settings rich in mood and tone, which might better serve as settings for the great theatrical productions of the time, whether new works or Shakespeare. Craig patented an ingenious system of movable and foldable panels that afforded an infinite number of combinations; in combination with light projections and shadows, they could be used dramatically and effectively for the staging of plays. He sold his idea to the Moscow Art Theatre and its director, Konstantin Stanislavski, and the panels were used in the Theater's 1912 production of *Hamlet*. "There is a persistent theatrical myth that these screens were impractical and fell over during the first performance. This may be traced to a passage in Stanislavski's *My Life in Art* (1924); Craig demanded that Stanislavski delete the story and Stanislavski admitted that the incident occurred only during a rehearsal. He eventually provided Craig with a sworn statement that the mishap was due to an error by the stagehands and not the design of Craig's screens."* Later, Craig

*Christopher Innes, *Edward Gordon Craig*, Directors in Perspective (Cambridge: Cambridge University Press), 1983.

E. G. CRAIG.
STAGE SCENERY.
APPLICATION FILED APR. 27, 1910.

1,022,020.

Patented Apr. 2, 1912.
4 SHEETS—SHEET 3.

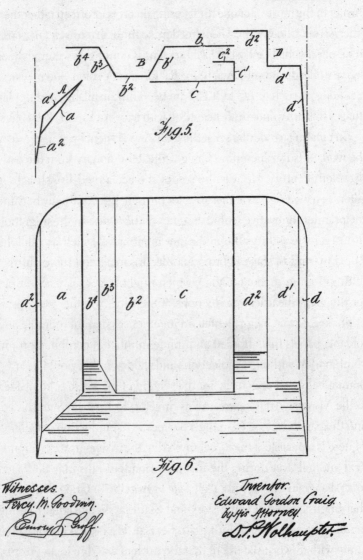

Fig.5.

Fig.6.

Witnesses.
Percy. M. Goodwin.
Emory L. Groff.

Inventor.
Edward Gordon Craig.
by His Attorney.
D. S. Wolhaupter.

A page from Gordon Craig's original patent application

sold the panels to Yeats and Lady Gregory at the Abbey Theatre in Dublin, where they were used successfully for years.

My thought was that perhaps these modular neutral walls might function as a set for the UCLA workshop. Easily moved and with panels that folded in both directions, a group of them might constitute a labyrinth with infinite possibilities for shots. They posed a special challenge for live presentation because they had to be especially easy to move. But also I liked the fact that they could be slid in and out of shots in the creation of those images. If I said I wanted a window here, or a door there, or wanted stairs to protrude, this might be easily accomplished using the panels. We built a number of units much in the way Craig had envisioned, and added more, with doors and windows (interior type on one side, exterior on the other), resulting in a total of 29 units. These, along with set dressing curtains and props, were the only settings used in the UCLA workshop.

I had built a scale model of the Craig panels with small magnets on their bases and could plan by setting them on a metal base.

The neutral off-white panels, with their endless possibilities of flaps opening and closing, provided many scenic configurations. It was literally a maze, but the two-way folding panels allowed actors to make exits and entrances, cameras to lurk, and new scenic situations to be quickly created with the mere opening of a flap. Thus the Gordon Craig patent answered my need for modular settings. Certainly, with the great possibility of projections and lighting elements shot onto the off-white walls, many textures, ambiances, shadows, and moods could be achieved. One could say that we combined use of the Craig panels with Adolphe Appia–type effects (image and graphic projections on scenery). We had a foldable, easily swiveled labyrinthian setting that would yield hundreds of sets, and could differentiate them with projections, shadow, and other effects.

In a true commercial production of my script *Distant Vision*, which is set in a tenement from the 1920s, I would have wallpapered the panels and perhaps added other details as a setting for a tenement party, but I did not in this experimental workshop, so I could use those panels for other scenes.

In addition, realistic effects seem possible: the shadow of a banister, or light from an exterior element, brick and stone textures, all have potential to be tried. Another possibility might be that these panels could be aged and textured as with normal sets, yet still retain their modular function.

THE SHOTS

It was quickly evident that despite the intriguing folding flaps and walls which afforded good means to hide cameras, and although the main shot being constructed might be very optimal, with perhaps a second and even a third shot from the same axis, many shots were compromised. The best reverse angles, even close-ups, couldn't be shot live within the group of cameras focused on a scene, for the simple reason that the cameras were not invisible. This led to any number of shots which, while useful, were not the best I might have wished. Our cinematographer, Mihai Malaimare, Jr., was ingenious in setting the seven or more cameras covering each scene for various shots, but I realized that though they might be fine for the workshop, I would not be able to get the angles I really wanted. As with so many things, there was a good and bad to that, because some of the compromised shots, being less than typical, were more interesting. Yet, I'd say definitively that this is a problem with Live Cinema: you cannot easily get the best shots you wish for all at the same time. There were some possible solutions for this problem, such as the 4K camera I mentioned previously, and I took those when there was no other way to get the shot I wanted.

One solution was to pre-shoot the shot, record it on the EVS, and then use it during the performance with the scene playing live. This worked fine. During the performance I could cut between the live cameras, which were labeled by number 1, 2, 3, 4, 5, etc., and use the EVS for any specials that were needed, those being labeled A, B, C, D, E, and so on. In live television, nomenclature is important because you're making choices quickly and you don't want to confuse what's live and what's pre-recorded. If you said EVS 3, it might be mistaken for 3, which is a live camera.

What happens if your story requires scenes at the beach or other locations that cannot be faked either by stagecraft magic, Translights, digital motion-control, or green screen? Even in Hollywood during its own Golden Age, one tried to shoot as much as possible at the studio, on sets, exterior or interior. Each studio maintained extensive picture libraries so they could research and recreate any period from anywhere in the world. It was thought that what they couldn't build at the studio, they'd cover with a few days or weeks of second unit, shooting at the actual location. The studios had giant backlots, following the tradition that began with D.W. Griffith's *Intolerance*, and the backlots continued to be used throughout the '40s and '50s. The Hollywood formula for filmmaking was simple and effective: you built sets either in the studio or on the backlot, so the great majority of shooting could be done there, certainly when the expensive principal actors were being scheduled and under conditions you could control. The few scenes that really required a unit to shoot in a distant location were done there, second unit, sometimes with doubles wearing the stars' wardrobe. Often this could be accomplished in a few weeks and with very few people—none of them with big salaries. The Hollywood formula is one way Live Cinema can be approached. But now, with nearly instantaneous communication across the globe, other solutions are possible. For example, productions can originate from a distant location, or two or three such locations, with the director and his team in the control room yet somewhere else. No doubt other technological solutions will emerge. Really, in a digital medium anything is possible, depending on the concept and the budget.

In 1964 I had the great privilege of being driven around the 20th Century Fox backlot before it was destroyed to make way for Century City. It was thrilling; I passed large settings for *The Song of Bernadette*, and *The Robe*, and other films. Throughout all of Hollywood, one could find similar amazing edifices on the backlots. And the sets built inside the studio soundstages were often as impressive. Although I must admit I was as a twenty-five-year-old filmmaker most disgruntled when Warner Bros., due to a tiny budget, turned down my request to film *Finian's Rainbow* on real tobacco-growing locations in Kentucky, despite the presence of the great Fred Astaire as well as Petula Clark and Tommy Steele. As a result, I was forced to shoot on the reclaimed interior and exterior settings of *Camelot*.

The answer to this question of how to deal with expensive or exotic locations is simple: if you have sufficient budget to shoot on location, you can do so; or you can pre-shoot shots with live integration and editing at a later time, even making the location shots available via satellite, or in conjunction with other scenes being produced live in the studio. Whether you make Live Cinema or traditional cinema, the issue of studio versus location remains the same.

6

THE SHAME OF THINGS TO COME:
MADISON, WISCONSIN

Someone I consider a friend is California Governor Jerry Brown, who was also a friend and colleague of my brother, August Floyd Coppola. I stress my brother's entire name, because my own really was a copy of his. I always loved how my brother's name looked all together, and so I used "Francis Ford Coppola" in imitation of him. At any rate, we were friendly with Governor Brown, and on that basis, when he asked me if I would film a sort of commercial for his 1980 run for President, I said I would—but I thought it ought to be a live event. This turned out to be the most embarrassing and disastrous experience of my career—though it says much about my feelings about television, and live television in particular.

The Shape of Things to Come was an early attempt at a live political presentation. The idea was to show Jerry Brown appearing live in front of the state capitol building in Madison, Wisconsin, giving a speech on live television and underscoring that with images that portrayed the goals and dreams of America as he spoke. We were faced, of course, with a limited budget, and I had never done anything like this before. A television company was contacted in Madison, and arrangements were made to rent a video truck that could handle the five or six cameras we were able to rent, along with the operators and staff necessary to operate them. I worked with Jerry on his remarks. I had him dress in a trench coat against the weather (it was March), and then sourced a number of supplemental sources, including films like *The Plow That Broke the Plains* (a 1936 short documentary film by Pare Lorentz with vivid imagery showing American farmland) so that occasionally I'd be able to switch between this footage and the cameras showing Jerry in front of the large crowds the event would attract.

As usual, I made the whole project as difficult as I could, with ideas to enable live television not only to illustrate what the candidate was saying with stirring images, but to use chroma key (there was a screen behind Jerry) as well to superimpose him over the images that would intensify the optimistic notions he was presenting. I prepared the source materials, brought them with me to Wisconsin, and loaded them into the facility of the rented TV truck. A helicopter with camera was engaged to shoot this impressive scene: the illuminated building with a rostrum before it seemed ideal, making it appear as if Jerry was already President, speaking to an excited gathered crowd. Governor Brown stepped out in front of the Wisconsin State Capitol, looking "presidential." So did the building, which houses both chambers of the Wisconsin legislature along with the Wisconsin Supreme Court and the Office of the Governor. The edifice exudes power and could be a stand-in for the highest halls of power in Washington, DC. Governor Brown approached a platform with bunting fluttering, in frigid weather, wearing his trench coat. It was my intention to make full use of the fact that it was cold outdoors, as live political statements were rare at that time.

One thing I tend to do is bring a concept as close to the brink of failure as I can, and by doing so learn what can and cannot be done. It was no different in this exercise in using live television for political purpose: I wanted to see how far I could push it. And indeed, I pushed it beyond my capabilities.

Inside the truck, horror struck me as we prepared to go live: the images before me on the preview screens were live with the rented cameras, but the images were all the same. Each showed a view

★ **THE SHAPE OF** ★
THINGS TO COME
★ GOV. EDMUND G. BROWN JR. ★

★ FRIDAY (MARCH 28th) 6 PM ★
WISCONSIN STATE CAPITOL

OUTDOORS
★ **A LIVE TV EVENT** ★
DIRECTED BY FRANCIS FORD COPPOLA

★ **!!! COME !!!** ★

PAID FOR BY BROWN FOR PRESIDENT COMMITTEE

of a man's legs and feet aimed toward the ground. Frantically I addressed the cameramen through the intercom to lift those cameras and find the angles I had already discussed with them. But the intercom didn't work. The operator of the truck tried to turn it on, but the images persisted on the screens of only the cameramen's feet. The clock ticked on and we were live.

I switched to the aerial view of enormous crowds as the candidate stepped forward to the speaking platform, but there were no other shots to cut to. Finally, I saw that one cameraman had focused on his shot despite the lack of intercom communication; the others oddly just had their cameras aimed at their own shoes. The speech began, and I was frantically trying to reach the ears of the cameramen to give me shots to choose from. But there were none. So I rolled *The Plow That Broke the Plains*, with its stirring images of America, and for lack of other shots, decided to ask the truck to composite the Governor's image over these images. The result looked as if it were coming from Mars, with the chroma key distorting and providing bizarre and unusual effects over Governor Brown. The intercom never gained functionality, and I did the best I could with what I had, but the result was probably the weirdest political speech ever given. As it all concluded, I remember swearing that if I ever attempted live television again, I would have a truck that was fail-safe, and above all, an intercom system that worked.

Mind you, Jerry Brown was most generous when it was all over; perhaps he hadn't realized what a mess it was. He was most kind, and in fact, years later when he ran for Governor of California in 2010, he and his gifted wife Anne Gust came to me to ask if I'd assist in making his political messages. I did, and he was elected. But I was always grateful that he didn't hold the poor results of that first live television ad against me.

When the original experience was over, I decided later on to shoot *One from the Heart* as a form of live television, but my memory of the rental truck and crew's failure prompted me to build a video truck of my own to use at my new Zoetrope Studios. I chose a self-propelled custom version of the Airstream trailer, one of two they built, the other being for NASA.

I recall the thrill of seeing the completely outfitted unit (eventually named "The Silverfish" by the boys from the 1983 film *The Outsiders*) being driven into my new studio blaring "Ride of the Valkyries," that triumphant music from Act 3 of Wagner's *Die Walküre* (and *Apocalypse Now*).

7

ONE FROM THE HEART:

ITS LESSONS

The story behind the intention and making of *One from the Heart* is interesting, and a single decision I made as we approached the beginning of production remains one of the few regrets I have in my long life. But there is something that I learned from that decision which influenced me later on during the two experimental workshops conducted at OCCC and UCLA.

Around the time that I began thinking about the film in the early 1980s, *Apocalypse Now* was in the theaters, and had received what I thought was an undecipherable reception from critics. Frank Rich of *Time* magazine had greeted it with a review in which he called it "This decade's most extraordinary Hollywood folly." The film opened at the Pacific Dome Theater in Hollywood, where George Lucas and I had marched down the aisle prepared to be knocked out by *Lawrence of Arabia*, and despite the mixed-to-negative reviews, audiences in good numbers were going. The film received two significant technical Academy Awards in 1980 (for cinematography and sound),* but was outdone for Best Picture by *Kramer vs. Kramer.* Since I was the principal backer of *Apocalypse Now,* which had gone over budget by costing about $32 million, at a time when interest rates had gone as high as 21%, it seemed to me that in time I would be financially wiped out. Moreover, I felt I would be discredited artistically, after a run of projects that were deemed immense successes: *Patton, The Godfather, The Conversation, American Graffiti,* and *The Godfather Part II.*

No one had wanted to finance *Apocalypse Now,* and none of the actors I had discovered and worked with in those previous pictures wanted to be in it, until finally, Marlon Brando agreed to do it for $1 million per week and 11.5% of the gross. I remember driving to Malibu and having some interesting conversations with Steve McQueen, but in the end he sadly told me he couldn't leave his family for so long and dropped out.

It's helpful to understand my feelings about *Apocalypse Now,* which was probably the most daunting and terrifying experience, both artistically and financially, I have ever had. It was clear that I had flown, like Icarus, too close to the sun, and it was only a matter of time, whether months or years, when I would experience a great and final fall. With that in mind, I felt perhaps I could quickly put together another kind of film, something surefire that would be so entertaining and popular that when the final devastating failure of *Apocalypse Now* arrived, this new film would save me. With that

---

*Vittorio Storaro for cinematography, and Walter Murch, Mark Berger, Richard Beggs, and Nathan Boxer for sound.

I began to think about a comedy, even a musical comedy, a form which was not looked upon favorably in those years.

A nice-looking young man, tall and dark-haired, by the name of Armyan Bernstein, approached me one day at LAX airport, asking if I would read his script. This is something that happened to me often, and as I more than anything wanted to consider myself a writer, I was never interested.

His script was called *One from the Heart*. It was set in Chicago and told more or less his own story about the relationship with the girl he loved and lost. I liked the idea of doing a love story, especially one that was a comedy, but I really wanted to do a musical. I felt the time was right for that once-wonderful Hollywood form, which, like the Western, was impossible to even talk about to the studios, who were always looking for something like the last hit. Everything else was usually *verboten*.

In those days I lived in San Francisco with my young family. I had a beautiful penthouse office on top of the historic Sentinel Building in North Beach, and had collected ownership of a number of buildings in the area, including the wonderful Little Fox Theater. I owned a weekly magazine, *City Magazine*, which was draining what funds I had left, and I had recently bought a radio station, KMPX. It was a dream of sorts to do creative work that spanned all these mediums: stories could be published in the magazine, performed live at the theater, and subsequently broadcast on radio. I don't know exactly what I was thinking, but it was an exciting time for me.

I knew, however, that the debt from *Apocalypse Now* was looming and would become my own financial apocalypse, and I was scared. So I did what I always do when I am frightened, which is to pose some newer, bigger, more daring and exciting project to leap into. I had another idea that was infectious: I could have a studio within a city, right there in North Beach. One building would be the story department, another would be the acting department, yet another across the street would be a cafe, and to the left of the theater would be the film and sound laboratory. All of this in a real neighborhood with a Bohemian tradition and peppered with good restaurants, cafes, hangouts, bars, and possibly even girls. It was what I always wanted: *la bohème.*

I saw *Apocalypse Now* revenues trickle in, but felt it was as close to the failure I dreaded as could be. I didn't yet have a script of my own, but the one I had in mind, which I called *Elective Affinities*, had been conceived as a cycle of films, a quartet about love, suggested by Johann von Goethe's timeless novel of 1809. Each of the four films would be a season—spring, summer, fall, and winter—and each film was to portray an aspect of the love proposition as an element in a chemical reaction: the man, the woman, the other man, the other woman. *One from the Heart*, the script the young man gave me, had something of an aspect of this plot, and I began to think perhaps that the script could be a musical. Maybe instead of Chicago, I could set it in Las Vegas, as the story was about the greatest gambling any of us would ever do, finding and keeping a beloved. Little by little I convinced myself that an urgently needed shortcut to my goal might be to grasp Armyan's script, integrate it somehow into the *Elective Affinities* scenario, and make a commercial musical comedy that would save me from the inevitable *Apocalypse Now* avalanche that was coming down on me. No doubt I was crazy to think this way, but that is my recollection of how I was thinking.

Meanwhile, my effort to pull together the idea of a San Francisco studio was frustrated by what I felt was a hard-nosed resistance; landlords wouldn't sell or lease adjoining properties and wouldn't cooperate with my imagined studio within a city. I became frustrated. The inevitable fallout coming from my perceived failure of *Apocalypse Now* would soon be upon me.

To make things more complicated, MGM, the studio that owned the rights to *One from the Heart* and was willing to produce and finance it, had certain limits. The budget was modest, and they didn't particularly see the need to make it a musical or in fact to make any musical at the time. And they didn't understand why I wanted to set it in Las Vegas. I'm not sure Armyan Bernstein did either, but he was so glad that his pitch to me in the airport had worked that he went along with the idea.

That's when I did a complete reversal: Why not give up the idea of a city-studio and buy a real Hollywood studio? There were a few on the market. I'd be located in L.A., where all the resources were, as well as the acting talent. For the money I had invested in the various San Francisco buildings, I could buy the Hollywood General Studios—where some of the final scenes of my favorite film, *The Thief of Bagdad*, had been shot at the beginning of World War II, where in my imagination Sabu, the young Indian-American star, had ridden tigers. It was arranged that I see the studio. I went through the gates, the same gates I had peered through longingly as a thirteen-year-old student at nearby Bancroft Junior High. I walked to the end of the lot, passed nine stages, and out the gates. I had decided. It would become Zoetrope Studios.

Then my imagination went into overdrive. In *Apocalypse Now*, everything we did was done the old-fashioned way, helicopter by helicopter, explosion by explosion. Now a new era began to dawn that would take the cinema to an entirely new place: the digital revolution. Movies would become electronic after all, just as I had always imagined. My new Zoetrope Studios could be the studio of the future, with a network of Xerox Star computers stringing all the departments together. The idea of a network never had been possible, but thanks to the extraordinary work of Xerox PARC, which George Lucas and I had visited, it was possible now. I explained to my colleagues that the network would be like a long clothesline that went into the windows of the story department and then out and in through the art department and so forth, until it passed through every department: casting, sound, effects. One could clip a story title and idea with a clothespin and yank the clothesline so it went into the story department. I could only afford two of the Xerox Star computers, and they were later repossessed, but at least I bought from Xerox rather than "borrow" from them as did both Apple and Microsoft. When Steve Jobs accused Bill Gates of stealing from Apple, Gates replied, "Well, Steve, I think there's more than one way of looking at it. I think it's more like we both had this rich neighbor named Xerox and I broke into his house to steal the TV set and found out that you had already stolen it."*

Zoetrope Studios would be the first electronic movie studio, ultimately with digital cameras, editing machines, and projectors. And that wasn't all. It would combine the future with the past, and would be run like the old Hollywood studios, with contract actors who benefited from acting, singing, and dancing schools right there. Young junior high apprentices would come in through the gates to work a few hours a day in the subject of their interest: acting, art, sound, music. It would be a kind of paradise—if only I could pull it off before the grim reaper of the *Apocalypse Now* reality could be beaten to the punch.

It was then that I proclaimed that I would do *One from the Heart*, set it in Las Vegas, and I compromised with myself by making it a semi-musical, not with the actors singing songs, but with Tom Waits and Crystal Gayle, singing an original score as "musical narrators."

*Walter Isaacson, *Steve Jobs* (New York: Simon & Schuster, 2011), 178.

Just reminiscing upon all this is making me excited once again! No matter that I really didn't have a bulletproof script; and of course I didn't want to do something so logical as just go to Las Vegas to shoot the story; I wanted to produce and execute it live, do a live performance much as John Frankenheimer did in the Golden Age of Television. I realized that at that time, this being 1981, there did not exist a television camera that could replace film negative and fill that important role, that of the camera. But I could and *did* fit the viewfinders of our standard film cameras with television cameras, so although the master negative would remain the standard 10-minute reel of film, I could see, edit, mix the sound, add music, and produce it live at least 10 minutes at a time.

When I was a UCLA student back in 1961, I was given the wonderful opportunity to visit Paramount Studios to watch Jerry Lewis direct a film called *The Ladies Man*. I always liked movies he directed and starred in because they were eccentric and did unexpected things. I remember that it was his birthday when I visited his set, and as always, I was ravenously hungry. It was memorable because there was an enormous birthday cake that was to be cut up and eaten, and it was a chance to see the amazing set of a girls' boarding house with the fourth wall sliced away. I also got to see his brilliant use of TV cameras mounted on viewfinders and recorded on 2-inch Ampex video recorders—so he could review the last take he did on a playback. Eventually, the big cake was cut up. I got as close to it as I could, and I tried to be courteous and kept handing off the slices to the folks not fortunate enough to be as close as I was. Of course, when I handed off the last slice I realized the cake was all gone, and in the end I never got a bite of it myself. But I always remembered his viewfinders and video recorder and wondered why that idea was never used afterwards by anyone else.

Now *One from the Heart* would benefit from this idea, and as a result the whole industry would learn, from my failed experiment, to use video assist.

We had nine big stages at the studio, and my great production designer Dean Tavoularis and his team filled them, one by one, with their replica of Las Vegas. It was a sight to see: stage after stage of large and spectacular sets representing—no, not representing—the art department had *built* Las Vegas, complete with its overwhelming neon reality, right there in this old studio on the corner of Las Palmas Avenue and Santa Monica Boulevard. The sets were arranged in order of the progression of the scenes, which meant the actors could go from scene to scene, performing the script live, with the songs being performed live, with final editing, special effects, and sound effects added live. Or so I thought.

What followed was a good example of how when a group of people are listening to a new idea each of them is hearing something different. Vittorio Storaro, no doubt one of the greatest living cinematographers in the world and a wonderful man, who had slogged it out with me in the jungles of *Apocalypse Now,* and who had shot Bertolucci's beautiful *Il Conformista,* came to me and said in his charming Italian accent, "Francis, why do we have to shoot with so many cameras, it is so hard for me to light. If we use only one camera, I can go very fast." And it was then that I made the decision, the only real regret in my life. I had bought a studio and filled nine stages with sets of Las Vegas (when the real Las Vegas was only a 45-minute flight away), I had done all of this so I could shoot *One from the Heart live*—to fulfill my life's dream to do Live Cinema. And because I cared so much for Vittorio, and probably also because I was so frightened of what I was attempting to do—I caved in.

MORAL OF THE STORY

Apocalypse Now never did reach the financial ruin I was trying to avoid; but *One from the Heart* did. People never stopped going to the Cinedome Theater to see the Vietnam film, which eventually paid for itself despite the 21% interest, amazing as that is. But *One from the Heart* turned out to be like that ping-pong shot your opponent smashes down to the table, which the critics did, resulting in two episodes of Chapter 11—reorganization of a debtor's business affairs—turning my family's financial life upside down. My wife and I were taken into a bank boardroom in New York with a large circular table, and were made to spend all day signing hundreds of documents, turning the entirety of our assets over to the bank, necessitating my spending the next ten years making one assigned movie each year.

And I never got to try my hand at Live Cinema.

8

RIP VAN WINKLE

After my financial fiasco with *One from the Heart*, I resolved to gain whatever experience I could in the medium of live TV. In doing so, I would accept any proposal so that I could learn and even try out ideas to see how it could be different from conventional theater. One opportunity came in 1987 with Shelley Duvall's *Faerie Tale Theatre* when Fred Fuchs, her producer, offered me the chance to do one of the shows in their series. The shows were shot in a continuous continuity and not actually broadcast live, but rather what's called "live to tape." Nonetheless I thought it would be a chance to work in a medium as close to live TV as possible, and see how the form was different from theater and film, the only two mediums I had worked in. Having produced Paul Schrader's excellent film *Mishima*, which featured the startling images of designer

Eiko Ishioka, I was also curious what a collaboration between Eiko and myself could accomplish.

Of the scripts I was offered, "Rip Van Winkle" seemed the most interesting, and I was anxious to see how well I could do with this classic story. I tried as best as I could to give the story an imaginative style using theatrical devices. For example, to depict the element of the mountain in the Hudson River Valley, I staged a group of actors huddled with a blanket over them and composited it into the scenery, so that the mountain could shiver in the cold and wilt in the heat. At the same time, I attempted to understand and make use of the technology unique to television.

The show ended up pretty weird—and while I never really heard if it was liked at all, my impression was that it was considered just that, weird, and the reaction was not the best. But "Rip Van Winkle" remains my lone commercial foray into something akin to the live television tradition. After many years of wondering how okay or just plain bad my little venture into Live Cinema with "Rip Van Winkle" was, I just did come across this notice by one Ignatiy Vishnevetsky, which appeared on the A.V. Club website:

Having re-watched "Beauty and the Beast," I decided to finally check out one of the last episodes, a handmade "Rip Van Winkle" directed by Francis Ford Coppola with Harry Dean Stanton perfectly cast in the title role. Of course, I'm now kicking myself now for not having seen this delightful and goofy piece of small-screen art earlier. With its primitive video effects and the faux-naïve, theatrical production design by Eiko Ishioka, "Rip Van Winkle" is a crayon sketch for *Bram Stoker's Dracula*. Not coincidentally, the two were produced by Fred Fuchs, who became president of Coppola's Zoetrope Studios after *Faerie Tale Theatre* went off the air.

9

THE QUESTION OF
STYLE IN THE CINEMA

There are any number of styles one is able to choose in the movie business—as long as it's *realism*. Maybe I'm being sarcastic, but it is quite rare that a producer and financier will willingly go along with a director's choice to work in an unusual style unless that director is so "hot" that they may work however they wish and with whatever style they choose.

REALISM

Realism has always worked to blow everything else off the stage, cut everything else out. At the end of the nineteenth century, realistic painted sets and lighting came to dominate the way plays were pro-

duced in America, as when James O'Neill toured the states with his stage adaptation of Dumas's *The Count of Monte Cristo*.

The following account, as told in Robert M. Dowling's thoughtful book on Eugene O'Neill, chronicles the story. "With sole proprietorship of the play as of the 1885–86 season, James O'Neill [Eugene's father] would perform the role to packed houses for almost thirty years," Dowling wrote, "earning him a profit of nearly forty thousand a year. Like Edmund Dantes, James had escaped from a prison of his own—the prison of poverty." Not all of his 6000 performances were praised, however. On December 31, 1887, *The San Francisco News Letter* wrote a less than favorable review of O'Neill:

"In his hands the romantic story has degenerated into an extravagant melodrama. . . . He is reaping the pecuniary profit of his business sagacity, but it is at the cost of art." According to Eugene O'Neill, "My father was really a remarkable actor, but the enormous success of *Monte Cristo* kept him from doing other things. He could go out year after year and clear fifty thousand in a season. He thought that he simply couldn't afford to do anything else. But in his later years he was full of bitter regrets. He felt *Monte Cristo* had ruined his career as an artist."

I find it interesting that the theater in the late nineteenth century was formulaic, just as our studios' films have become. This was evident in the scenery, in that everything was as real as could be in a proscenium stage. You can understand why O'Neill's playwright son, the only American dramatist to win the Nobel Prize in literature, wanted to free the theater, to bring everything back: masks that the Greeks had used, soliloquies, choruses, asides, mute shows, epilogues. It was inspiring to me because Eugene was a play-maker who wanted the American theater to be reborn. Channeling his

father's frustration, he would cast aside the constraints of "realism" and "selling out," while turning his life into art. How moved was I when I read: "Some of the earliest words O'Neill remembered his father uttering were 'The theater is dying.'"

Cinema, like theater of the late nineteenth century, is now completely codified, so that no matter what you do, it will immediately be assigned to a genre. Now in the Netflix and online content era, these classifications are used to rate and access films, and usually the lists of choices are offered by genre: drama, comedy, horror, romance, and so on. Further classifications may go to screwball comedy, coming of age, suspense, mystery, etc.

As to the style the filmmakers may have chosen, there remains— as in theater at the turn of the century—the all-powerful realism. The early German cinema was long on expressionism, the French and Spanish worked in surrealism, and one might also say a film was in a theatrical style, or classic style. *Citizen Kane* possessed a theatrical style of its own that worked. I remember the producer Robert Evans always telling me, when I was working for him, that he wanted a "movie-movie" style, with elaborate camera moves and thrilling action scenes. At one point during the making of *The Godfather* I heard he was bringing in an action director to give the film more of what he craved, and I spent the weekend with my nine-year-old son helping me run after "Connie" (played by my sister Talia), hitting her with his belt to reinvent the scene where Carlo beats Connie, in the hope of forestalling the dreaded action director from actually coming onto *my* set. But no doubt there are many style possibilities the director may choose from, and I would think that they are all there to be used as well in the Live Cinema category.

Movies, especially as reflected by their art design and camera style, also fall into such categories as handheld look, classic look, elaborate moving camera look, or combinations of these, and the settings can be naturalistic, minimal, or expressionistic. Since the invention of the Steadicam, there is now the one-shot look. Prior to that ingenious device, filmmakers managed a one-shot look by using the camera "hand off," such as in the great Russian film *I Am Cuba*.

All this still applies to Live Cinema. However, each choice brings up the issue of how one pulls it off in this demanding format. For a handheld camera style, you'd only be able to use green screen chroma key with any number of motion-control systems, adding expense and complication to an already very complicated process. Any kind of constructed, textured, and painted scenic settings work as well for Live Cinema as for classic cinema. Theatrical settings can be used for live television, but become more problematical for Live Cinema, which is less forgiving about painted or theatrical-type sets. So whereas any type of style can be chosen, the actual implementation of a production in Live Cinema makes great demands and may bring problems to the effort. These are pretty much all solvable, but the continuity of live performance no doubt requires of the production more precision than conventional start-and-stop cinema. One experiment I was curious to do was to use the standard television stylistic devices: the two-box, three- and four-box so familiar on CNN, or the commentator with headphones explaining what is going on in a football game. I note now that I didn't try these devices in my UCLA workshop, so probably I felt this was too strong a TV convention to suit my purposes. I want to ruminate on this experience a little more to figure out if I know another way to make use of these devices without their being such an obvious reference to TV news and sports.

I'd say that Live Cinema demands far more precision than movies, theater, or television. In conventional moviemaking, there is always a succession of takes, which gives you the chance to get one perfectly. In theater, with its nightly performances, there are always the nights when the show goes wonderfully or terribly. In television, which covers the event, there is always alternate coverage that might catch what the intended shot missed.

I'd guess that extreme naturalism might be the most difficult style to work in for Live Cinema, because it depends on a variety of locations—places not easily constructed or evolved through compositing or special effects and really only achievable in conventional cinema by actually going to those chosen places and doing one shot at a time. Often those places are not close together, and Live Cinema requires they be not only close together, but arranged in such a way that the actors can move between them quickly one way or the other within the time of the performance. This was done in *Lost in London* by shooting the entire project entirely within a few blocks of London.

FURTHER DEVELOPMENT OF THE GORDON CRAIG PANELS

I still have the desire to take the Gordon Craig panels that I used at UCLA and create a way of thinking of the scenic component as being realistically textured, yet still modular. That would mean my settings would be assembled out of modular units, panels or flats that could, if desired, be painted, textured, or (using the many new forms of stagecraft) molded, vacuum-formed, or printed upon, maintaining the movability of the Gordon Craig idea, so that entrances and exits of actors and placement of cameras and lighting instruments could be accommodated. This is assuming that the unity of the overall production is not readily accomplished in a conventional set. Any story that plays mainly in a single set (*12 Angry Men*) or complex of sets (*On Golden Pond*) can be solved in the same way as conventional cinema, with perhaps the addition of some pre-shot footage (stored on playback servers like the EVS), even pre-edited supplementary sequences.

In any case, the essence of cinema is montage, and the shot is the basic unit—and that determines for me how I would manifest the style of future projects.

MONTAGE

Shots are like subatomic particles that behave in many different ways, depending how aggressively you use them and at what temperature. The fact that you have isolated the work to its basic units liberates the way you choose to put them back together. The shot implies and necessitates that you do something with it. You now have something that you can build with, and you can begin to express ideas and emotion through the magical world of montage. Now that we know it is possible to view the Live Cinema performance as an accretion of many defined and specific shots, it would be a sin to not use them as parts of the cinematic language of montage. With coverage of a drama, your choices are limited: view the person who is speaking or listening, see the whole group when it's best to follow their action. The choices are few, because the shots are only coverage of the elements of a scene—not true shots that are composed to stand on their own. Certainly, shots are like bricks in a wall, and you can build a logical sequence of events, going in order, each one supplying a bit of the information of the whole. In the early silent films, that is precisely what was done. For example, James Cruze's *The Covered Wagon*, the epic 1923 story of wagon trains making their way west to Oregon and California, was told one shot at a time, occasionally with a superimposition of shots, but each shot was the part of the story relevant at that moment. The shots revealed the action: they gave us a grasp of what was happening, and the ability to understand what would happen next. The tempo of cutting might quicken as the action did, but generally one shot following the next gave you the unfolding of the story.

In Sergei Eisenstein's *October (Ten Days That Shook the World)*, a film that made a life-changing impression on me, shots are used in a number of ways and with different purposes, and the effect at the time of the movie's appearance was so dazzling that Eisenstein was catapulted to the forefront of cinema in the 1920s.

At the beginning of *October*, the statue of the Czar is shown in details; we see shots that break up the statue into discrete parts, almost in a cubist approach. Then the shots immediately begin a cause-and-effect mode, in which ropes are being pulled. Next, the shots are used to illustrate opposites in a sequence of comparisons: rifles compared to scythes. Almost illogical repeated action is then employed, the Czar's chair falling over, in a sequence of shots, with time repeated. Then there are many close-ups of men singing, then shots of men intercut with shots of war explosions.

My point is merely that once you've reduced the possibilities to discrete shots, you are encouraged to then do something interesting with those shots rather than just let them be units of the progressing action unfolding. In *October*, montage takes the path of using the shot to make comparisons—wide shots cut against very close shots, rich people vs. poor people, and so on. Now that you're working with unique shots rather than coverage, you can begin to use them in a variety of ways; repeated close-up (CU) shots of people waiting

at the railroad station to build suspense, letting the audience think "Why are they waiting?" Then suddenly, medium shots of search-lights and then the title card "It's him." And this is paid off with a dynamic shot of Lenin and the red flag. Now just shots of flags and banners, carefully art-directed: "Down with the Proletariat" intercut with "Down with the Provisional Government." The breakup of imagery into dynamic shots provides the ability to range through the multitude of possible ways to put them together. Very fast cutting, machine gun with rich lady; you almost think you hear the rattle of the gun purely through this illusion. The famous bridge scene of

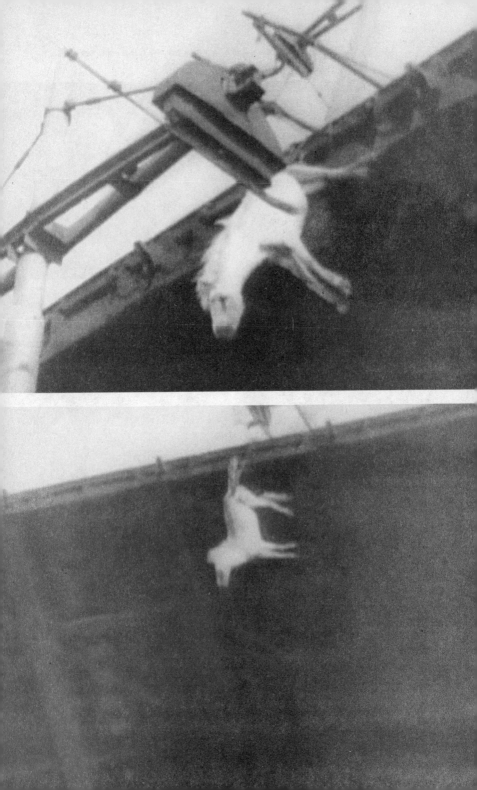

the film uses montage to expand time, opening in degrees. It's not merely covering the opening of the bridge: the shots are controlling the opening of the bridge in degrees while you keep your eye on the dead horse. Your emotions are stimulated as you know eventually (in time) the horse will drop off the bridge, which it does in a beautiful moment.

The point is that once you break the action down into discrete and well-composed shots, you then have the ability to recombine them into a multitude of different patterns—enabling many different emotional reactions and responses far beyond what you could do if you merely broke a scene into its components and followed the obligatory rules of coverage. If you break water down to some atoms of oxygen and hydrogen, all you can make out of them is water and maybe hydrogen peroxide—but if you can break those down into protons, electrons, and neutrons, you can make anything!

Thinking in terms of shots and their participation in montage is liberating:

In the sequence where Kerensky (head of the provisional government) waits, we cut to a statue of Napoleon and crystal glasses and decanters. Then Kerensky crosses his arms. A crown cuts to a whistle (you can hear the screeches even though there is no sound). Then: Church, Icons, God, GOD. Laughing Buddha, ancient, bird of prey, monster, primitive, models, epaulets, return of the Czar statue—reconstructed. Eisenstein is using a cinematic language to give his opinion of Kerensky. He cuts to a crown, Napoleon, Kerensky, Napoleon looking at himself. Shots of tractors, gears of tanks, more tanks, whistle, smoke, locomotives, train, newfangled armaments. Comparison of Kerensky's books against the counterforce of rifles and flags. Cinema is a new language in which shots are like words or sentences and can be organized, repeated, and compared at will.

THE STUMBLE-THROUGHS, TECHNICAL REHEARSALS, AND DRESS REHEARSALS

There comes a point when the well-rehearsed and energized cast of actors begins to stumble through entire acts, and soon through groups of acts, and, as soon as possible, the entire show. The process is very similar to what happens in theater, and the reason why I've chosen to have a theatrical stage manager calling the show. It is the stage manager's voice that warns of minutes until going live, gives the countdowns and the lighting cues, uses signal lights to deal with actors' entrances, and cues music and all the elements that will make up the show.

However, Live Cinema requires cameras, so it is the associate director and not the stage manager who is cueing them as to their positions, talking to them on the all-important intercom, and always one scene ahead, so that the cameras will be ready. There are any number of complexities when one is using a very large number of cameras (we had forty at UCLA). The associate director helps each camera operator by providing a card to mount on his or her camera with a list of that particular camera's shots. That way operators immediately know what the next position is that they will go to after their camera is finished for a given scene.

Television cameras of the type used in live television shows, as in sports and award shows, each have a device known as a tally light. I've never used professional TV cameras for reasons of cost, size, dependence on zoom lenses, and the fact that they are 30p (the standard frame rate for U.S. television). However, a tally light would have been a great convenience at UCLA. The tally light merely indicates on the camera which camera is currently online or being used. If your tally light is on, you as well as the actors and crew know that this camera is online and shouldn't be moved or readjusted, and the actors need to continue in character until the light goes off. I look forward to having the benefit of tally lights in the future.

In the first stumble-through and subsequent run-throughs, it is often unlikely, or even impossible, that the actors will be able to get from scene to scene in a timely manner. There are many tricks that have come to us from the Golden Age of Live Television, and they're all fair game. For example, when, during a scene, the shot is cutting between the actors speaking to one another, often (on *Playhouse 90*, etc.) the shot will remain on the final actor talking to his counterpart; meanwhile, the counterpart has run away and is frantically having her wardrobe changed, a robe or jacket added or removed while the previous scene is still going on, and as she's allegedly being talked to. As a result, she is ready to be there for the beginning of the next scene, which might even have further padding by beginning with a new character talking to himself essentially before she arrives.

There are other techniques for smooth transitions between scenes:

- One can use the EVS replay server to get the first few shots of the oncoming scene, and play them out, giving the transition more time to be accomplished.
- The entire oncoming scene can be pre-recorded on EVS servers so you are hopscotching from live to EVS to get through a difficult sequence due to extensive wardrobe changes or such.
- The new scene can begin on the back of an alternate cast member dressed to double the incoming cast member, enabling a transition in time.

It was my belief that sports' extremely reliable and instantaneous EVS replay servers could be used to great advantage in Live Cinema, and so I tested some difficult situations in which they could be used. One was in the need for many extras, including babies, children, and animals, which can add a lot of expense and require a great deal of supervision. The many dressed extras needed in a period scene such as the one we explored at UCLA would require teams of wardrobe, hair, and makeup people; animals require handlers, and children are the domain of the state, whose representatives supervise their well-being, work hours, safety, and education. Babies may only work for 20 minutes a day (if you have twin babies, you can thus eke out 40 minutes), and only within specific times of the morning and afternoon. I wanted to see how I could manage period scenes that had many extras, including children, a baby, a dog, a cat, and a goat (in my story, the goat was a gift from an uncle in the Bronx, intended to be eaten at a baptism party, brought by two brothers on the subway). My question to myself was this: could I have one day with all those elements, and the accompanying hair, makeup, and wardrobe teams as well as the state supervisor of children and the lunches for large groups—only one day, so I wouldn't be required to repeat all that for each day beginning with the stumble-throughs and technical and dress rehearsals? Could the football-type EVS machine make this possible?

What I learned was yes, one can intercut a live scene with the replay servers at will. At first it was difficult and tricky for my associate director and technical director to do this, but soon they were doing it fairly easily. On the multiview screen before me, I saw the many shots from the live cameras, and below those, the shots of the replay series. As I explained before, the live shots were numbered (CAM 1, CAM 2, CAM 3) and the EVS units displayed were (A)lpha, (B)aker, (C)harlie, etc. I found I could indeed cut whatever live scene was going on with the shots recorded on the EVS from that day when I had all those extras, animals, and kids. In fact, I did one scene with the big group, which was an improvisation of all those people wandering around the rooms, eating, playing with the kids and the goat—and even that was possible to use cuts from, giving the scene about to go on live the sense it was happening in the midst of all that crowd.

I am still evaluating the result of these effects, but I'd have to say that intercutting live cameras with playback servers appears very successful. This means that one wouldn't have to have all that assembled expense on hand every day of the stumble-throughs, tech rehearsals, and dress rehearsals. One wouldn't even need them for the final performance.

The one stunt we did at UCLA involved a boy being pulled by a falling radio antenna and falling from the roof. The story depicts two brothers who are early ham radio operators and have installed a kit that enables an early form of television. For a while they have it working, but there are loose wires to the antenna on the roof, and the older brother goes up to fix it. Ultimately this leads to a tragedy in which he falls through the hanging clotheslines strung between the tenements, and to his death. It could have been recorded on an

EVS channel, but I thought that the fact that the cast and crew knew we were going to do the stunt live at the final performance would excite everyone, myself included, and so we did it that way. As with the baby and goat, having a live stunt like this was a way to ask this workshop to discover what it could and couldn't do.

MARKS AND OTHER SMALLER
UNRESOLVED PROBLEMS

The two experimental proof-of-concept workshops I conducted, at Oklahoma City Community College and at UCLA, were based on different samples of my script, and had different objectives in terms of exactly what I wanted to learn.

In Oklahoma I wanted to learn about cinema-style lighting: could it be placed entirely on the floor, and how could we use the new LED battery-powered lights in this scheme? I also wanted to learn if we could even do a complete performance of a roughly fifty-page script, and what was necessary to build shots as one does in film production. At UCLA I wanted to learn how modular settings (Gordon Craig panels) would function, and also what uses we could apply to the sports-style EVS replay servers. To what extent would a fully programmable mixing board like the DYVI switcher facilitate the difficult juggling of so many formats: live cameras, EVS servers, pre-cut sequences, green-screen composites? Could I shoot one day of many dressed extras, animals, and children and intercut live scenes with those elements? Could I have scenes in a foreign language (Neapolitan dialect) with ongoing live subtitles, and could I integrate a live stunt? As a result of these two workshops I came to the conclusions I've tried to discuss in this book.

The answer to most of my questions was "yes."

The biggest problem I encountered in the OCCC workshop was cable management on the floor—sorting out the tangle of so many camera cables. The difficulty of camera placement was simplified by the lack of actual sets. The biggest problem I experienced in the UCLA workshop was camera placement. Frequently, optimal shots were not possible, and I had to settle for side angle and profile shots; true reverse shots were almost impossible. These issues were solved by pre-shooting reverse angles and using them in tandem with the live cameras. Importantly, I learned that it wasn't daunting to intercut live cameras with EVS servers. And I learned that live stunts were no more difficult than they are in theater.

I discovered the need for an important new crew job: a cinema-style script supervisor who operates the EVS "IP Director" program to be able to quickly locate shots that were recorded earlier, or were from previous technical or dress rehearsals. In addition, I learned that the very important areas of sound recording, Foley work, sound effects, live music, and sound mixing essentially behave as in conventional cinema, with the obvious difference that sound must be synchronized or performed during the live performance.

With the choreography of many actors and camera positions constantly changing, marks—indications of where everything needed to stand at the various points in the story—resulted in a vast collection of multicolored points and arrows on the stage floor. These were obvious and apparent in all but the lowest camera angles. Since

much of my story took place during a celebration, I chose to allow confetti to be sprinkled down from the grid, so that it would decorate the floor. While it didn't hide all the many colored marks on the floor, the confetti served to disguise them and keep the viewer's eye from singling them out.

The confetti solution may (or may not) have worked in the experimental workshop, but it certainly didn't solve the question of marks in future Live Cinema productions. I considered a number of other solutions, for example, marks in invisible paint that would fluoresce when under black (ultraviolet) light. I had even found very small UV flashlights that I thought the camera crew might carry, although this would not help the actors, who also needed to see the marks. Finally, I just ignored the problem—and hoped the confetti on the floor would be sufficient to disguise the marks.

At this moment, I'm still not sure how to fix the problem of marks. Perhaps there's another way of marking positions that would be invisible to the eye—magnetic, textural, or some other means. I feel confident that once I find myself attempting Live Cinema for real, I'll come up with a solution to eliminate the thousands of colored angles and lines that decorate the floor.

I'm trying to think now what other unresolved problems I found along the way, but I come up with nothing—other than the sheer immensity of the number of pieces one must juggle to do such a production. At one point five days before the broadcast, my technical director (TD) Teri Rozic, who's among the best there is, told me that in spite of the fact that our program was only about 30 minutes long, she thought I really should have had two TDs and two associate directors (ADs) to handle all the tasks. From Teri herself: "Here is how I can imagine two TDs working on a project like this. There would be a lead or main TD who would be the one to figure out all of the moving parts and how to put them together. They would be the primary operator of the switcher and therefore do the live switching. A second TD would help in the massive amount of programming, primarily the multiviewers." It is a great feature that the EVS switcher can have multiviewers programmed per scene (stage), but it is a tedious process that requires a great deal of time, time that needs undivided and uninterrupted attention.

Then, during the show, the second TD could be responsible for following along with the show and routing the correct multiviewer layouts at the right times as well as helping to get the next scene (stage) ready. If I had had a second TD at UCLA I would also have had them cue my playbacks. As Teri told me, "It was too much on my plate to manage the multiviewers, cue the numerous EVS clips for roll-in, and keep my brain on the show to do what was meant and not what was said. If I were to do it again I would not have all of the playbacks that were rolled in under my complete control."

I find myself still thinking about what that could mean— you might divide the performance into two leapfrogging video units, having each TD and AD handle 20 or so minutes, and then switch to another duplicate unit, enabling the first to reprogram and prepare for the next?

It reminds me of how old movies were shown, 20 minutes on one projector and then a changeover to a second projector with the next 20 minutes while the first projector was threaded up with the next reel. I doubt that alternating video units will ultimately be necessary, considering the nature of the digital controls and the potential to program the controls to handle vast collections of shots and sounds, but if it is necessary, how ironic that the most modern and sophisticated electronic cinema would need to copy the old changeovers of the classic motion picture projectors. Some things never change.

12

OBSTACLES AND OTHER
THOUGHTS ON LIVE CINEMA
NO MATTER WHAT THEY MAY BE

have essentially discussed everything I have on my mind regarding Live Cinema, and everything I've learned during the two
experimental workshops. Having thought a lot about all these
things, I must ask myself, do I still want to do it? It's a lot of work,
a lot of worry, and the result may not have clear advantages over
conventional cinema. With the control you have in conventional
cinema, perfection is only a matter of your imagination and the
financial and production resources you have at your disposal. Aside
from saying that at least you have "true performance" at the heart
of this new form, the response may be, "So what?"

Why might Live Cinema be better? I find this difficult to
answer. When you look at an on-screen live performance and a
recording of it, there's no difference whatsoever between the two.

In the recorded version one is tempted to correct any mishaps or mistakes—sometimes as easily as merely replacing the flawed part with the section from a previous dress rehearsal. So one difference between the two forms is that the recorded and edited version is perfect, whereas the live version may have flaws. I think this is good. Flaws in Live Cinema are like the intentional mistakes in the weaving of Navajo carpets so the evil spirits can get out, or in Persian carpets, so as not to offend Allah, alone who makes perfection.

As I mentioned earlier, one solution might be that the director of the Live Cinema production could intentionally cultivate flaws by lacing the live performance with obstacles. This is something that Spike Jonze seems to have done on his YouTube Music Awards show of 2015. It was a live show, and my nephew Jason Schwartzman was one of the hapless hosts. For starters, the hosts didn't really have a script or a true roadmap of the show, only some index cards that they could follow. That was already a form of obstacle in that no one was really sure which card would be selected and which way the show might go. Then at one point, without warning, a mother plopped her year-old baby into Jason's arms (an obstacle). He then needed to move ahead with this little life in his arms, not at all sure if the baby would cry and squirm or remain content. Throughout the show, various other obstacles were provided: In a scene where it was necessary for the actor to climb up to a higher level of the set, the stepladder that always had been there was removed. Within the chocolate layer cake there was an important clue, but the knife that was always there had been removed, and the two hosts had to destroy the cake with their hands in order to get the clue. These suddenly unplanned-for tasks had to be dealt with, and you could see the panic on the actors' faces as they tried to carry on, not at all sure things would work out. In short, the idea of obstacles as a pre-planned gift of the director to the actors was used to wonderful effect—and certainly made the live broadcast, including a spectacular dance sequence by Greta Gerwig, something very different and enjoyable.

Perhaps, I thought, that is the secret of directing Live Cinema and getting something conventional cinema cannot: by using deliberate and unannounced obstacles, you can invite panic, difficulty, and even failure, periodically treating the audience to witness the actors struggle to get up to the higher level of the set without the stepladder, or observing other moments of embarrassment and struggle. In other words, this sort of becomes a *Candid Camera* approach, as in the old Allen Funt show, which caught people in awkward situations on TV.

I must think about that the next time out.

13

EQUIPMENT—NOW
AND IN THE NEAR FUTURE

Television now dominates entertainment around the world, with yearly symposia and trade fairs attracting millions of eager buyers. NAB Show, the annual trade show of the National Association of Broadcasters, offers the chance to examine and consider adding the many technical developments to the hundreds of thousands of broadcasting entities. In the centers of television production throughout the world, and concentrated in major cities, exists the technical capability to control and manipulate image and sound to a degree that would never have been imagined fifteen or twenty years ago, and at a steadily decreasing cost. The NAB show's tag line is "Where content comes to life." So be it.

CBS, the company with one of the best technical and research traditions, thanks to the great work of its technical director emeritus Joseph Flaherty, was the first to adopt video cameras to replace

16mm film cameras for news gathering. The company has for decades conducted research and development in collaboration with Sony and a full gamut of other Japanese equipment manufacturers, as well as with NHK, Japan's public broadcasting company. Barry Zegel, Senior Vice President and General Manager of CBS Television City, told me that they are equipping their massive studio in Los Angeles with new 4K cameras and are currently contemplating the use of several 4K cameras stitched together to be able to cover sporting events with the ability to derive any shot they may require. CBS Television City opened on November 16, 1952, and was where much of our television history was made, including my favorite *Playhouse 90* production, *The Comedian*. Today they are investing time and money in the facility to provide digitally built scenery with motion control capable of being used in live production. There is virtually no area in the production of television today that remains untouched by the kind of engineering that brings with it new possibilities.

Arri, synonymous with nearly a hundred years of movie cameras, now makes thousands of digital cameras per year, although it still makes the necessary parts for its famous Arriflex film camera, which it will assemble only on the basis of an actual order. Arri's digital cameras have become a mainstay of the film industry (which, ironically, no longer uses very much film). New camera companies such as RED and Blackmagic offer sophisticated digital cameras for both movies and television, while Canon, after discovering that many filmmakers were using its still camera to record movies, now makes an affordable camera for that purpose, and Sony Professional builds some of the highest-quality digital cinema cameras in the world.

Presently, there is a declining number of film directors who have the desire and clout to be able to still shoot film: Steven Spielberg (who edits on film as well), Quentin Tarantino, Wes Anderson, Christopher Nolan, and my daughter Sofia are a few. Film is photochemical, requiring film, laboratory developing, and printing on film, while digital video records signals sent by an imager, but both use lenses, which is where the real beauty of the recorded image lies.

PHOTOGRAPHY IS AT ITS APOGEE

In 1977, Polaroid founder Dr. Edwin Land (though he never completed his undergraduate degree, he was called "Dr." by his associates) introduced the Polavision instant movie system. The product was a financial failure, and in 1982 Polaroid accepted Land's resignation as chairman. Around that time, I decided to try to find a rare copy of Johann von Goethe's early-nineteenth-century book on color theory with color plates, and contacted Dr. Land's office to see if I could visit him at his Polaroid headquarters in Cambridge, Massachusetts, and present him with a gift. I knew that although the Goethe work on color ultimately was discredited and replaced by Isaac Newton's (much earlier) work on color, Goethe's scheme had been helpful to Dr. Land's early work in two-color photography. The Polavision unit had a small camera that accepted a special cartridge which, when played back on an accompanying viewer, would instantly develop the film and show you color movies. It was similar to an 8mm movie camera roll, producing about two and a half minutes of silent movies which could only be viewed on a special desktop viewer. My son Gio loved the Polavision. He experimented and played with it— it produced a unique type of colored movies instantly. But I had my eye on the new unit Sony was making, their electronic Handycam camera, which connected by cable to a small mobile recorder and produced an hour and a half of video movies with sound. To me, the writing was on the wall: the electronic system would be the death knell of Polavision. And ultimately it was. But I greatly admired Dr.

Land and wanted to meet him and express my gratitude for his great work, and to present him with the Goethe volume as a gift on the occasion of his leaving the company he had founded.

I took a flight to Boston especially for this purpose, and was delighted to find that Dr. Land was waiting for me. I ended up spending most of the day with him. He was very kind, and seemed genuinely excited when he unwrapped my gift—and noted that of course he was familiar with Goethe's work with color, and that it had definitely been useful to him. We spent the day touring his facilities, and his own personal lab. I remember feeling a great respect and sense of history as he took me through the lab where many experiments were still underway. As he showed me around, we discussed the factors that had ultimately led to his decision to resign: primarily, the failure of Polavision to capture the market. Everywhere we went were stacks and stacks of colored Polaroid SK70 photos, all of beautiful Smith College girls posing to test the color balance and flesh tones. I thought if I were he I'd be testing color the same way. It was an extraordinary experience. He'd shoot a laser at some distant target in the dark, and it would respond with a brilliant flash. Or he'd show me the enormous prints his company had made of art masterpieces, reproducing them with uncanny fidelity.

He told me that his company originally thought they'd make their fortune with Polaroid glasses for 3-D movies. But each time a 3-D trend began after a particular movie—*Bwana Devil* in 1952, *House of Wax* in 1953—the fad died out, and their bonanza selling the glasses never materialized. He even said he had invented a new 3-D process in which the emulsion on either side of the celluloid base of the film was polarized in different directions: only a single normal 35mm projector was required; the projected film, when viewed with the Polaroid glasses, would appear in three dimensions (previously it required two projectors or alternation of small frames of the two images). He said the Disney company had made a test of a cartoon this way. (I later contacted Disney, but they had no record of it. Nonetheless, I eventually found an independent expert who actually had the sample of the process and loaned it to me. I threaded the single reel of 35mm film on my projector and tried it out. It worked great.)

In the course of this wonderful day with this brilliant and wonderful man, I finally brought up what I figured was a taboo subject: the new video cameras that were appearing on the market, and had no doubt a part in dooming Polavision. He sighed and finally whispered sadly, "Ah, but photography is at the apogee of its development."

I certainly can understand. Photographic film's beauty and luster are a great achievement; film is a link to the great cinema of the past, of Kurosawa, Ray, Ozu, Murnau, Fellini, Wyler, and Bergman— and it has a look of its own, imperfect, but an imperfection that is beloved. But there is no doubt in my mind that the digital image now achievable will continue to improve just as film did over the years. At the end of the twentieth century there may have been doubt that cinema would be electronic, edited on computers, shot on digital cameras, and projected by vivid, bright digital projectors. There will always be filmmakers who wish to continue shooting and editing film, but fewer and fewer, until the issue will become, "Where does one buy and develop film?"*

THE STEADICAM AND LIVE TELEVISION

The Steadicam, which was introduced in 1975, is an invention that enables a person carrying a camera to produce smooth, floating, steady shots without a dolly, tracks, or other complications. It is a system of bal-

---

*Film will, however, continue to be made for archival and other purposes.

ances which the operator supports by his body, so that the camera floats wherever he walks. When used in a live television production, such as *Grease Live!* (2016) or *Lost in London* (2017), it can move through corridors, in and out of rooms, taxis, and cars, and precede dancers and actors as they burst anywhere they wish, even from interior to exterior, because it provides basically one continuous, fluid shot. It can also contribute many views, panning and tilting at the operator's whim, and producing long dramatic dolly-like moves without a dolly. A camera mounted in this way can make a shot that would otherwise require many cameras and editing. It is an effective tool in a live production, with few of the complications present in multi-camera sequences.

The Steadicam was used magnificently in the Andrea Andermann production of Verdi's *La Traviata*, which was staged in 2000 as a live television performance in real locations in Paris, beautifully realized and photographed by Vittorio Storaro. The Steadicam was operated exquisitely by Garrett Brown, who invented it. Garrett also was the principal camera operator on *One from the Heart*, which used the Steadicam extensively shortly after it was invented. Garrett is a big strong man, and as can be imagined, a fantastic Steadicam operator. What he and Vittorio did in *La Traviata* is extraordinary, moving in mirror-clad rooms without ever being seen in reflections, while beautifully depicting the characters of the classic Verdi opera.

THEATERS AND HOMES—EXHIBITION

If you're not familiar with professional movie theater 35mm film projectors, certainly you've seen scenes in movies like *Cinema Paradiso* that show large machines rattling away with big spools of film unwinding by the glare of an arc light. The projector in the local movie theater is no longer a film projector requiring nine or ten reels of film delivered to the theater, loaded up and projected, switching from reel to reel. Film projection is now either fed by a locked hard drive (until a time when the cost of the projectors has been retired), or receives a feed by satellite.* Is the content going to remain as it was when it was alternately projected 20 minutes at a time, because that was the length of the reels? Will theater owners really be able to insist that they have a window of four or six weeks when only *they* can show the film, with home viewing withheld by edict of the theater owners?

I've always been impressed that pretty much whatever the customer wants, the customer gets. I know people love to go to the movies in theaters, as I do; but they also enjoy having the right to view entertainment on a television, computer, tablet, or phone, anywhere they wish. They may see a movie in the theater one evening, and see it again at home with their kids. Who knows? It's up to them, and so it will continue to be.

Furthermore, it's very hard for me to accept that after the transition into the digital realm that has happened with *all* of the tools necessary to make movies—with the lone exception of the lens—that all that can be different and yet the movies tend to remain the same.

THE GREATNESS OF TRADITIONAL CINEMA

The wish for movies to remain the same is understandable. The motion picture is roughly 120 years old. There exists not *one* greatest film ever made, or ten, as someone or some organization is always trying to list, not fifty, or one hundred. There were already perhaps thirty great masterpieces made in the silent era alone that are still

---

*Neither the exhibitors nor the film studios want to pay for the installation of new digital projectors in theaters, so a third-party investment entity gets a percentage of the tickets until the cost is retired.

beloved. The sudden appearance of sound stopped short the appearance of masterpieces, and sent cinema back to recording stage plays for a while, but the development soon began once again.

I would guess that there are many hundreds of film masterpieces. Kurosawa alone probably made nine out-and-out masterpieces, Fellini a half dozen, and so on. These were anywhere from ninety minutes to about three hours long, mostly but not entirely shot on black and white film, with a narrative structure constantly being improved upon, and with beautiful performances from the cast. After many years, color film came to replace black and white, although we now still find a place for both, depending on the theme and style. Kurosawa made many masterpieces in black and white, as did Fellini and Bergman. Antonioni made beautiful films in black and white, but then he made *Red Desert*. Bergman made *Fanny and Alexander*, and the color was original and superb. Heroic work in saving our film heritage is being done by Martin Scorsese, founder of The Film Foundation, as they endeavor to preserve and restore many classic films.

I've often wondered about this burst of creative greatness—why and how it happened. My only conclusion, however romantic, is that during the nineteenth century the unconscious urge to make cinema was present and building—but the technology simply did not yet exist. Goethe, who was born in 1749 and died 1832, was a man of his time—a poet, novelist, scientist, playwright, and theater company manager; but I'm certain he would have jumped at the chance to make movies, as would his colleague, the dramatist Friedrich Schiller. Richard Wagner would have found cinema a natural expression of his music-drama concept. Playwright August Strindberg would have as well. Wagner's great Italian counterpart Verdi owed much to Schiller, whose plays were the basis of at least four of Verdi's operas. So by the time that motion picture technology did become available, there was a surge of creativity that gave us wonderful cinema, to be added to the world's great literature.

Yet this burst of cinematic work presents something of a slight problem. These films are so moving, so wonderful, ingenious, and convincing, that all young filmmakers, including those in my own generation, could set their aspirations on nothing higher than to try to make a film that was in the vicinity of such great examples. One dreamt of making a film "like" 8½ or, in my case, like *Blow-Up*; of doing something more or less like *The Best Years of Our Lives*, or *A Place in the Sun*, or *Singin' in the Rain*—and so on.

So does the fact that we love these old films to the extent we do act as a barrier? That sometimes we don't even try to think beyond them, even when the means to manufacture them has entirely changed? It's as if having the technology, we build an airplane, but insist on driving it around on the highway because the cars of our time are so wonderful and beloved.

A NEW INSTRUMENT

Sometimes I wonder, what would happen if there came into existence a totally new musical instrument, one that didn't depend on human breath or reeds or brass, stroking or plucking strings, or banging on hides? Something totally new, with sounds that only recently had arrived from heaven, with neither keys nor theremin antennae, an instrument absolutely new that no one knew yet how to operate? How long would it be before some damn fool came along and tried to play it? And if that happened, would the intrepid instrumentalist insist that the resulting music need sound like music that came from the traditional orchestra? Or does a new instrument imply new music? And how do you get to new music when the old music is such a treasure, and all anyone wants to create is something like it?

WHY AM I DOING THIS?

I n *Live Cinema and Its Techniques* I've explained how I conducted two experimental proof-of-concept workshops, one at Oklahoma City Community College and one at UCLA. I based them on different excerpts of my script-in-progress, and had different objectives in terms of specifics I wanted to understand. But I haven't yet discussed much about my script and why understanding Live Cinema is truly so important to me personally.

I have always loved when art works *are* what they are about. To me that is the holy grail of art, but perhaps I've only touched on it briefly. The making of *Apocalypse Now* reflected many of the same elements that made up the Vietnam War: youth, abundance of equipment (firepower), rock and roll, drugs, an out-of-control budget, and naked fear. It *was* what it was about. I think of the extraordinary life of Yukio Mishima, the great Japanese novelist, whose entire body of writing paralleled the essence and precise facts of his life, ending, in fact, in a sequence that might very well have been out of his writing, where he staged a right-wing coup with his private army, and ended his own life with ritual *seppuku* (suicide). His life and death *were* as much his art as was his brilliant writing.

Several years ago, realizing that I was now of an age when it was time to begin an ambitious project that could serve as the culmination of my life (if there is such a thing), I ranged through all sorts of possibilities and then came upon a thought. Certainly Fellini had made his work a unique reflection of his life with 8½; but even before, his *La Dolce Vita* had so *nailed* that period of the 1950s that if a Martian were to come to earth and ask, "What can you tell me about the fifties?" all you'd have to respond with is, "See *La Dolce Vita*." It was all in that film: the point at which "celebrity" had eclipsed Christ; the advent of the paparazzi; the futility of one's work at a time when it meant nothing in terms of the transitions going on.

At this juncture, I began to wonder if there was a single theme that I could appropriate for my own era: the post–World War II era, when so many interesting things seem to have turned our world upside down. It was the time of the Cold War, a renewed effort to attain civil rights, an age when man went to the moon; our era was defined by a senseless war in Vietnam, by the sight of a popular young president slaughtered before all of our eyes. We had experienced all those things and more, I realized, through *television*: it was the television era, which was launched in black and white and became color as we watched. Television began even to define who we were by reflecting who we were.

So I began to feel that all I could do as a culminating work was to look at something like my own family: perhaps several generations of it, as the young Thomas Mann had done in his magnificent *Buddenbrooks*; and in telling my own story, I'd be telling television's story as well, because in three generations of the Coppola family the entire history of television—its birth, development, and the beginning of its destruction (or transition to the information age)—could be told. And then it occurred to me: I must tell and fictionalize this story about me, my family, and television in a new art form that is the progeny of television, film, and theater—Live Cinema. Just as *Buddenbrooks* was the story of several generations of the Buddenbrooks (really, Mann's family) during a time of seismic changes in Germany, an era when the commercial confederation of merchant guilds (the Hanseatic League) that had controlled Baltic sea trade, gave way to a new German nation, something like my own family's saga over three generations would come to reflect the enormity of changes brought by television.

With this as a goal and Mann's *bildungsroman* as an inspiration, I began to lay out the structure for a big cinematic work dealing with three generations of the Corrados, loosely based on the Coppolas, that would begin just as television was first emerging, and then develop as television came to be the dominant force of the period. So for me, there was no other way to express this: it had to be done as "what it was about," in a new form of television, which I have been discussing as Live Cinema.

In my studies, I was very impressed, as you've come to realize, with the ambition of young Eugene O'Neill, who wanted to see a flowering of American theater, which he believed had become stagnant. In the 1920s he reached out in many directions to incorporate traditions that had been lost, at the same time using using his own personal life and his family's life in cycles of plays. And in doing so, he gave himself everything—sea—fate—God—murder—suicide— incest—insanity. I too felt that if I were to spend the time looking at a family like mine, I wouldn't be able to tell the stories in just one cinema play, but would need any number of them to contain all I felt there was to tell.

My script is now very long, and far from done. It's called *Dark Electric Vision*, and is currently made up of two cinema plays. The first is titled *Distant Vision*, followed by *Elective Affinities*. My dream would be to produce this work at a facility like CBS Television City. My intention is to do each play live, and beam it out to movie theaters around the world, making it available for home viewing as well. I'm told the great Noël Coward, later in his career, would perform in his own plays for only six performances. Taking from this precedent, I thought our own productions would give six live performances—including performances at different times on the broadcast days so they could be seen in other time zones around the world—available to theaters or home audiences. After the sixth performance, this life cycle of sorts would be available only as archival copies. Everything I've just spelled out will no doubt change. Whether this, or anything like this, is possible, I have no idea. Right now, as you have witnessed, I'm busy trying to set down what I have learned from my two workshops—from camera angles and marks to the immense logistical and financial challenges of such a massive and ambitious production.

Truly though, the main unanswered question remains: would anyone want to make Live Cinema other than me? How shall I answer this? It is exhilarating and exciting to work in this new form of cinema-television-theater. It is unquestionably, indubitably the logical emerging offspring from these three parents: theater, film, and television. I would guess the answer is *yes*.

Francis Coppola with the cast and crew of the UCLA Live Cinema Workshop, July 22, 2016.

JOURNAL NOTES DURING OCCC
LIVE CINEMA PRODUCTION
MAY/JUNE 2015

In Oklahoma, I kept a daily journal. At UCLA in Los Angeles, a year later, I did not. I'm not sure why exactly—perhaps because in L.A. I was on familiar ground, and had friends and relatives to connect with. Thinking that this view into my daily morning thoughts during my stay in Oklahoma might be interesting to the curious reader, I've included it here.

MAY 2, 2015

Here in my new apartment in Oklahoma City—very spacious, good kitchen, good situation in a quiet bldg. near lots of activities walking distance. Gym and pool upstairs. Now I slowly need to reduce bric brac and move my own stuff in. I have my boxes to empty and situate myself. Secret now is to calm down, settle in—relax and eventually start thinking about rewriting SHORT DV to get it to highest potential to learn from. I have a place, a car, a studio, Silverfish and staff so all is coming together and is in order. Now I need to put my exercise pattern together, and do my workout here in bedroom, and then think about gym upstairs and if that is an option.

The 7X is in the hangar here and the pilots are in training in Dallas, quite close. Soon, Anahid, Masa, Jenny, Robby will be here, Gray is already here.* Step by step takes me where I want to go. Best thing is just to look around, check the closet space and keep my boxes, storing owner's bric brac in them, storing them. Seems to have much potential. Come one month, I will be a lot smarter regarding the subject of LIVE CINEMA than I am now.

Here's the just out cover of the Wine Spectator—I hope it's good for INGLENOOK!

MAY 3, 2015

Sunday. I just met with the costume designer Lloyd Cracknell, a very kind man, and I realized just what Jenny had told me, how much such a man appreciates and loves "family." He spoke so much about his nieces and how he takes each of them on a trip and about seeing his family at home in Cambridge. That is the thing people at large don't grasp; just because they are gay, doesn't mean that they're not every bit as involved with their families; their mothers and fathers and all the children of their siblings. Maybe more so. Of

---

*The names mentioned throughout can be found in the Credits, p. 165.

course they want unions under the conventional word MARRIAGE because they want more than anything to continue to tie with their families and be accepted and integrated as part of the family as they know it.

Beyond that, he was very suitable for what I'm doing here with SHORT DV and I was pleased to have him on our team. And further to that, I looked over the faculty of OCCC and it's extensive so I'm sure there are many other resources I can pull into the SHORT DV project.

All is well; I am here—now I must rewrite SHORT DV: be healthy (do exercises), work hard (write SHORT DV), be happy (pasta fazool).

MAY 5, 2015

My thoughts ought to return to SHORT DV and what I can do to make it more succinct and a better use of the experimental workshop. I have this hunch I can work in the marital troubles that Tony has more, off-the-cuff, more as if by accident, and right when something, some main thrust, is going forward. As if it happens in the middle of the LIVE BROADCAST and not really planned or part of the show. The wife comes into the Silverfish and interrupts the broadcast and they somehow have that scene about the "protégée" right when all this other stuff is happening. I will try.

Beyond that—I hated that AVENGERS movie and so the taste of the world and I are parting even further than before. Nothing I can do but note it is happening.

Also, Don Quixote is more entertaining than ever, what with each of his "Knight Errant" adventures ending up with him getting trounced and beaten up and Sancho coming out with the most ridiculous "sayings." It's fun to read.

Well, on to make the most out of this day.

MAY 6, 2015

For me, the truth is—nothing is more important than that 100% of my attention be given to SHORT DV because doing it will be more difficult than even I, typically oblivious to practicality, think it will be. It is, even at this scale, next to impossible. It depends much on cable management and keeping the different simultaneous layers of activity separate. Each layer makes sense so that they begin happening at the same time, occupying the same space as they must, they remain orderly. That is why this Stage Mgr. I am meeting for lunch must grasp how to do it—more so, have a natural comfort with how to do it, as does the TD Teri, who exists on the other end of the process.

MAY 10, 2015

Things are okay now in OKC—I'm comfortable in my Bricktown apartment; my little white car is ready and I know how to drive to the college. Masa and Robby will be arriving shortly and soon the Silverfish will be placed on the stage, I think.

So again, the most important thing is the script.

Here are a few points that Greg, the professor here I've chosen as advisor, has given me:

1. Since in this version it's really Archie's story, in Sc 7, when Chiara says she fell in love with Archie at 17—is there any way, either from her or through your exciting use of feeds, to give us a feel for why she fell in love with him, which also helps pull us in a little closer to Archie, seeing/feeling him through her eyes? (Archie dancing with Chiara when she's a young girl? Chiara putting his picture on her wall?)

2. In Sc 10 . . . maybe this is just a performance thing between you and your actors, but it seems like things go bad just a bit too abruptly. All I can do is draw from my family dynamic—and my father was raised in Italy and would have been a winemaker if WW2 had not come along, so instead he joined the Navy and then became an FBI agent afterwards.

   (This is Chiara's intro to Corrado household, the fight, etc. "Proof she's a virgin"—How can I make less abrupt?)

Would my family explode in a situation like this? You bet. But since what they would most want in this situation is to put a good face on things for this lovely new member of the family, my Mom and Dad would have fought against this explosion just a tad bit harder. Would it have gotten the best of them like it does in this scene? HOW CAN THEY REMEMBER THAT THIS NEW YOUNG GIRL IS IN THEIR PRESENCE? Yes! They would just have been fighting it, since it's the last thing they'd have wanted to put on display—on the very night they welcomed her in.

Maybe it could help Vincenzo too, our feeling for him. But this is my family, not yours, so trust whatever feels true to you. (?)

3. In Sc 14. . . how can Nadia Boulanger be more than just a name?* Maybe through use of a feed? Or something else? Can we get a feel for Archie's composer dream here, versus his flute world, which we get a good feel for? WHAT DOES NAME "NADIA BOU-LANGER" REPRESENT TO ARCHIE? (CARMINE) A DREAM NOT MADE POSSIBLE BECAUSE OF US KIDS.

4. In Sc 31, pg 20. . . Why is Archie being on his knees difficult to imagine? Can we have some beat with him before that lets us experience why this is true? I HAD FILOMENA ASK THIS OF HIM, WHAT ELSE COULD I DO BEYOND HIS JUST SAYING IT? This will also help set up that fantastic moment when he goes on his knees to offer up his dream if God will only let Tony walk again.

5. Sc 43, pg 28 . . . when Archie calls himself a shit composer, is there any feel possible for the kind of composer he is—before this? Maybe a feed thing at some point prior to this? It is Archie's major conflict, the flute versus composing. OK, HOW GOOD A COMPOSER IS IT? WE ALL HAD NO DOUBT HE WAS TALENTED—HOW TO SHOW?

We hear the flute. It would help to hear his music. GOOD POINT— Because in many ways his conflict is that despite how blessed he is with the flute, his passion is not for playing the notes others have found out there on the Creative Frontier. He wants to be out there on the Frontier as an explorer, discovering those notes himself. YES, WHY DOES ARCHIE WANT TO BE COMPOSER RATHER THAN FLUTIST? THE MONEY? THE VANITY? BECAUSE

*Nadia Boulanger was a great French composition teacher. Gershwin studied with her. My father always wanted to.

HE ALWAYS THOUGHT OF HIMSELF AS BEING A KIND OF GERSHWIN.

6. Sc 55, pg 33 . . . Maybe this is too much, but at the commencement last night I watched our music professor conduct his choir, and saw the energy the music and voices filled him with—enliven his body, his hands, his eyes . . .

ANOTHER GOOD IDEA—UNCLE KIKI SAID THE SAME, TONY OUGHT TO WATCH ARCHIE CONDUCTING!

Is there any way to get a last flare of light and feeling, very subdued since Archie is near death, but get that feel for that energy surging one last time through him as Archie imagines the music and orchestra coming together as one under his leadership—especially if this is something that he composed—his dream come true. MAYBE HE CONDUCTS THE ORCHESTRA THAT PERFORMS THE SONG THAT DOESN'T WIN.

And if he is conducting something he's composed, if that could be just a bit clearer somehow, that would be good too.

What's good about Greg's recommendations is that rather than being cuts, he's pointing out opportunities to get more out of the scenes that are IN the script already. Things I can deal with, by thinking about.

MAY 13, 2015

Now it's Wednesday, so I need to give Rachel (asst.) the tag for my trousers and ask her to pick up. I am rapidly approaching the first reading of SHORT DV here in OKC and am excited. It will be a day of work with the actors, first having them read the long script; then two readings of SHORT DV, first stop and go with discussion, and then lastly once straight through with no interruption.

I think I've pretty much covered everything; and Ellie and Gia seem up and proceeding. So now I should just relax, do my exercises, and make my way over to OCCC.

God is merciful, gracious, and creative and we wish to follow in those ways. Remember, every day make a fellow creature have a happy day.

quick journal: THINGS THAT COULD GO WRONG

— transitions not accomplished ON TIME
— bad switching because of me
— bad roll up on VT and VT PGK's
— bad sound—can't hear actors
— actors can't hear cues (mainly as with Tony in Silverfish and Darryl on stage)

MAY 15, 2015

Great first day (readings) of SHORT DV. Today is theater games and improvs—perhaps group improv going through "lunch" in which they prepare any number of the sets, and all visit each other's places (some sort of celebration) wherein they prepare cold cuts and other types of food, and eat and act together. All is well—the text has richness, humor, feeling. The final one could almost be ever ongoing: interesting.

MAY 16, 2015

Interesting day #2, many theater games, one improv: Archie first meeting Chiara as a kid. Then we did a big group improv on the stage, with the actors helping set up areas, and then each with the different objective I gave them, preparing and actually having lunch together while they were hungry. It was long, and there were a few nice moments. Filomena tends to talk too much, always trying to dominate the scene, whereas the real Filomena was taciturn, strong, and didn't need to talk too much.

All in all a good day. Now today (Saturday, Day #3), Mihai is coming, and I'll try to give the camera persons their assignment: (how to test), ask them to do a composition on a group of actors with a specific (the same) lens and judge, who did them best? And in order, assign one to Archie; one to Chiara—or premier principals, and then master shot, eccentric shot, moving shot, etc.

Tried to fall asleep last night with music but it never shut off and I was awake tossing and turning. Not such a good idea. Hope I'm awake today, as when Mihai leaves, we need to have a good idea of lighting philosophy and composition style. Also how to deal with b.g., as in Dogville, etc?

MAY 18, 2015

Today, MONDAY, I have to hit the mat hard and stage both part 1 & part 2 of the SHORT DV, and be pretty aware of the camera angles. So I should use my Leica finder. Maybe I ought to do a fast read-through while I ask Steve to lay out tables and chairs for all those scenes or be ready to do so after each one is staged.

This is my chance to catch up and be very SPECIFIC about the logic of blocking and camera shots. So far so good, I have done much in the first three days, so now it's Monday and DAY #4 and I must push forward.

Biggest dangers I see are lack of logic in scenes: why does Vincenzo's family show itself as so dysfunctional when Chiara moves in? What is Filomena's relationship to sons? (They all loved her, as did I?) If I get these two parts staged I can follow my original schedule. Cosima's sweet little 5th birthday, and now here's Pascale's as well.

MAY 19, 2015

Tuesday morning. I think the SHORT DV experiment is going well. Now my priority after I can begin to see run-throughs of the three parts is to devise the CAMERA LOOK, the shot positions. I am pleased with all the departments: props, scenic, lighting, music— now comes the TD today, and then step by step I am building this LIVE experience. I like the attitude and effort of all the student crew. So far, I must say, as of this writing, that all areas are as good as I could have hoped for.

The IDEA I had that still seems a good one is to let SHORT DV be the "hub" of DISTANT VISION. And let it grow like a snowball rolling down a hill, until it becomes the fully developed long project. Build outward from this center, and let it grow longer natural, under its own rules. Don't decide how many evenings it will occupy, rather keep working on it from this SHORT DV center, and see how large it grows.

MAY 20, 2015

So far so good. Now it's about DAY #7 and I have the SHORT DV on the main stage, just need to fix the "poker game" and Vincenzo alone in front of TV and I more or less have the basis for the "settings."

Met with Archie last night; perhaps Tony tonight. Maybe both Vincenzo & Filomena together—leaving only Chiara left.

Now hopefully Mike Denney will add logic to the "camera situation."

As I said, "So far so good."

MAY 21, 2015

Up early; soon I'll be at the studio to continue setting shots. This morning will start with the big dinner scene: fight, etc. I guess this part is tedious, but when I make an unusual shot it's then THERE and I can count on it coming up in the visualization of the story. Television AND this family.

I need to just keep going through and setting great shots.

MAY 23, 2015

Here's where I am: it's Saturday. I have all scenes except for: FFC walk from Silverfish, Christmas tape recorder; OFTH, Alison-Tony inside the Silverfish; Archie visits Tony/Alison apartment; limo (Western Union); limo, Archie conducting at awards ceremony and Archie/Tony in ambulance—with cameras added. I must finish today, so that in days to come I can do full run-throughs with cameras, plus adding costumes, makeup, hair, and final lighting.

I have to be especially practical today: knock off all the shots, while at same time making the style more dramatic.

MAY 24, 2015

(actual letter sent to all:)

> *Day off: SUNDAY*
>   *What I'm doing here could be best described: "What if" you had ALL the cinematic-style shots pre-laid out, shot-by-shot & lit from floor (not grid), and were able to have the actors move throughout them in a live performance—with all other elements: music, sound, lighting cues, green-screen composites, pre-recorded elements, graphics, and even time-manipulative expressions (replay, moving in time, etc.) also performed live—resulting in a cohesive dramatic production happening in real time.*
>   *So I am on schedule, and beginning Tuesday will run through the entire production (about 50 minutes) each subsequent day, with three commercial breaks, from beginning to end, each time adding a new level of finish—costumes, hair, final props, scenic elements, lighting cues, pre-recorded & graphic elements—until somewhere around June 1st I will begin dress rehearsals, until the FINAL DRESS, which will be recorded and mistakes removed by editing so it can run in tandem with our final performance, being a sort of safety net.*

*This "proof of concept" really is doing what I intended,
making it clear to me what the futuristic LIVE CINEMA
process is actually like and in what ways it differs from LIVE
TELEVISION of the past & even the present: It is what
I had termed "PRE-VISUALIZATION" 30 years ago, <u>but
where the Pre-visualization is also the final performance</u>, the
key difference being that it is performed in real time and
with SHOTS that are actual cinema shots and not formal-
istic "COVERAGE," i.e., Establishing, Over-Shoulders,
Close Ups, etc., and with lighting from the floor and not the
overhead grid.*

*Also, there is a new area afforded by actual LIVE switch-
ing within replay machines, offering an ability to manipulate
time while in fact time is flowing normally. This area is yet to
be totally digested and used to its advantage.*

*(Note: It depends on some degree of pre-design, although
the scenes can be rehearsed one after the other in a semi-scenic/
prop simulation not all finalized, with modular elements such
as "work" chairs, tables, apple-boxes and work props I have
been using. In a funny way it's not very different from Rawnsley's INDEPENDENT FRAME of the 40s, except once all
the details are noted, there is expressive freedom as the actors
travel through the sets in real time. The concept of the sets all
arranged around the perimeter of the studio, with a "free spot"
in the center where the equipment is based, accomplishes the
same as IF's sets all up before the CAMERA/LIGHTS rolling
on and off by rostrum?)*

*We begin our technical and dress run-through perfor-
mances next Tuesday—*

Sent from my iPad

I didn't really finish today's entry. I explained how my Live Cinema is nothing more than pre-visualization made animate. Between the previz phase and the performance phase there are weeks of rehearsal and shot layout with relevant camera angles—and then (magari!)* the film is performed. But it's not unlike Independent Frame in that the shots exist and the actors walk through them during the performance of the play. Anyway, having been immersed in the process, I am understanding how it works. And had I to do it again, I would know how. Although I must say that I anticipated much, and certainly put my "experts" in the right places.

MAY 25, 2015

OK, it's Memorial Day, and Gia has just left to fly to L.A. It was fun having her here with me, the little shrimp. Where am I? In Oklahoma City and ready to begin complete run-throughs tomorrow (Tuesday). Perhaps I ought to do a run-through in the actors room to just have them play, play and play the piece? Think about it.

However, the key for me is to focus on each day's plan. Early, get the actors in line rehearsals while tuning up the technical issues; get the intercom installed, and such facilities. Set up Brian's piano in the sound room. Set all the pieces and then do a complete stop-and-go run-through, and perhaps at 5:00 each day, a complete run-through with a new layer added: costumes, hair, final props, perhaps tomorrow record all the voiceovers in the sound room.

My mind is organized, so I'm sure I put the emphasis where it need be.

Remember, I can always pull a Van Wart and during a bad dress

*Italian: I wish.

make them do another after that, even going late (reward with some sort of food).

Technical shortcomings are more difficult for me to remedy, since I truly have no control over the machines.

MAY 26, 2015

Tuesday, "resume"—reading to go into DAY #10. This morning I plan to work solely with actors in the actors room while stage is left to the crew to organize themselves for an after-lunch adding of period CAR & AMBULANCE. Then 4:00 complete run-through with such elements as we have: cameras, VT, costumes?, props?, scenic.

All right, this morning is to focus on the actors, acting—the story and all that. Should Anahid be there with me? Or more valuable to plan VT segments. I guess the latter.

I think I have this on course, as well as the FFCp stuff. As I understand what Joe was saying, FFCp is the master company, and FCW under it. Thus, as we change FFCp (through a DBA) to THE FAMILY COPPOLA, it all eventuates the way I want it.

I seem to be hitting my stride: productive, energetic and juggling many balls in the air as well as ever I did. I think the exercise is part of it. Also being at peace with my wife by giving her what she wants: "A happy wife is a happy life."

MAY 28, 2015

DAY #12. As I watched SHORT DV, I despaired that the shots on Tony's Silverfish monitors weren't showing what I wanted them to show. However, now—if I prerecord most of the "source VT," and route them to screens in the EVS room, and have a camera there, I could essentially fake that those screens WERE the Silverfish screens and what both Tony and Darryl were looking at—and that Chiara was switching.

What I realize now is that the task of all that switching between the live cameras (with their number rename issue) was more complex than I imagined, even for a professional like Teri, and that the added burdens of chroma key, etc. make her job almost impossible, given the limitations of the TriCaster and the lack of graphics and other stations.

Today I should keep going through "blocks" of the script and confirm camera settings, confirm VT portions and settings, and continue going through a block at a time. Now I have roughly done that with PART ONE, so must continue with PART TWO the same way. Also, the intercom will be here and set up by late this afternoon— plus Mike Denney will be here, and I ought to have him sit in the Silverfish and work with Teri.

When Owen gets here, I'll get his opinion on how the overall piece is playing, ask for some suggestions regarding the OVERALL and which parts in particular he can help with.

It is exciting, a fantastic "machine" to play with. My actors are doing fine, oddly enough, especially Chiara, Vincenzo. What could give Archie more tragic stature? Ask him to play it as if he's almost cursed—by not achieving what his father wanted: more Greek Tragedy?

MARSYAS—SATYR WHO PLAYED THE FLUTE:

MAY 29, 2015

Main problems:

• SOUND. He has too much to do and is little experienced. Get someone else to be responsible for microphone placement and sound boom placement and instruction. Will should be at the control (mixing) panel.

a) The RF mikes should be mounted on a simple loop harness that can just be hung around an actor's neck or shoulder, and can come off quickly and replaced with the new costume quickly. (This should be done by the movie sound guy.)

b) Will should begin to actually do "sound design" by adding sounds, ambiances, and specific sound cues.

c) Perhaps Robby will have to start taking over some of that.

• STG. MGR. should stay at his station and run the show, all cueing over intercom. He should never be off intercom during the running of any act, and of course during the complete run-throughs. He has to mark lighting cues that he's giving to Sean. He may need other subalterns like Daniel, who floor-manages wardrobe, props, and scenic. Maybe two or three efficient guys to direct all that floor traffic.

THE STG. MGR. HAS TO BEGIN CONTROLLING, CUEING, AND RUNNING THE ENTIRE SHOW FROM HIS STATION, and ALWAYS ON INTERCOM.

• Brian needs to be set up in his MUSIC RECORDING ROOM with his piano, his script, and a BIG monitor so he can watch and perform as the show progresses. He ought to be on intercom during the entire show.

• We have a bottleneck to the TRICASTER, which means Teri needs a very efficient TD type who can handle all the patching, and sending the relevant cameras to the eight feeds of the TriCasters.

• It may be best to have Mike Denny sit next to Teri in the Silverfish, and act as Assoc. Director, and have Wendy on the floor working with the camera operators.

MAY 30, 2015

I slept worried that the SHORT DV was drifting into a movie set, with "just two minutes" expanding and eating up all the time, and Steve the stg. mgr. less adept in this type situation, off-intercom and failing to have his second stand by me. So I figured the smartest thing I could do was push it back into a theater setting, with him at his station and always on intercom during the show. I have Beggs as backup in case things go terribly wrong, sound-wise—and we'll hire a movie sound guy to set mikes as Will operates the mixing board and various cues. I have to weigh all things carefully as we now proceed into the week of run-throughs.

After rehearsal Saturday. 1 put them through the entire piece. Acts 1 and 2 were ragged but held together; act 3 hit the fan, and with so many cameras missing, was ragged. Tomorrow I should start with Part Three, and set each camera, and then record image on vectorscope. A lot rests on Robby—he's got all those pre-recorded sequences to cut, and his instincts aren't mine. That leaves SOUND—sound recording; sound mixing, all sound design, and integration into a single moody & legible sound track. (Beggs could do). We have nothing to fear except fear itself.

LAST THOUGHTS ABOUT DV RUN-THROUGH TODAY—If the cues are all hit, and you can hear and understand the dialogue, and if the music & live score is mixed in with some finesse, it will be an enjoyable experience. It is aggressive in how it took the bull by the horns, and made a dent in what LIVE CINEMA is and could be.

MAY 31, 2015

Sunday, early before I go work at OCCC on the "voluntary" day. I do feel this performance will come together—probably not until June 3rd, oddly, on Wednesday. But that is sufficient. Also, my hunch is that Beggs will show up; but I have to plan for him not showing up. What about Jim? Could he do it? He's comfortable with sound, so perhaps. Let me ask, but first see if I hear back from Beggs.

What is the vulnerability beyond the TriCaster crashing? Hmmm, it's that the thing plays in real time, and that transitions are instantaneous. I do think it's OK, however, if we "catch" the madness of the elements just being assembled, actors rushing in, sets being set, couches slid in those seconds before the scene begins. It is meta-theater after all—which those interviews with Chiara et al., polio discussion, all express.

So as good as we try to get it, that last-moment madness of even a camera still trying to set isn't bad, and it presents a further safety net. This is very exciting—and I'm glad I chose to do it and grateful I had the necessary $ to push forward and actually attempt it.

Step by step.

JUNE 2, 2015

OK—its Tuesday morning; I do the performance in three days, Friday at 5:00 P. M. I'd imagine there will be time for a rehearsal on Friday morning, but wonder if I ought to have a late morning Friday. What are the weaknesses? Getting all the cameras, sets, & costume changes between the scenes. It's now a totally technical issue in which a few days would make a big difference. If there are problems with the "show," I don't think it's in the beginning nor in the ending. Maybe around the FFC intrusions, which we've never done—and we should shoot that at least for the Thursday schedule. Idea: Should it be Archie who closes the curtains, as he runs out with Willie earlier than Chiara? Or get the closing of the curtains VT by Chiara? How much time would it really gain? Also, how about some fingers pushing switch buttons VT, so we can have such shots? What other inserts—the ax in wood pile?

List of INSERTS:
- Tony's fingers pushing switcher buttons
- Ax in pail of wood, being pulled out?
- Chiara closes curtains
- Vincenzo's glass rapping on table (when he's blind)

<u>Of all my problems going to performance, the actors are the least of them, lighting little; most is moving all the cameras into place, on time.</u>

Reaction to the run-through: Occasionally there were touching moments, interesting or exciting moments. What can I do with Alison? Other than underplay? Make her energetic re: her work. How do I get her to stop "acting"? She has to be worn down by the conflict of work and marriage so that she almost has no emotion anymore. She should play the scene with Tony in the Silverfish AS IF:—she's closing a deal;—telling someone she loves to take it or leave it;—she's gotten news that she's got a month to live;—gotten news he's got a month to live;—feels she's already lost him;—she's about to tell him about her own affair;—she's Judge Judy;—she's a minister;—she must feign concern or emotion. Even anger: she should strip down to the essence of her feeling, be bare, be naked—remove her protection.

JUNE 3, 2015

There were two run-throughs today; the first camera/actors/scenic improved, whereas Robby playback (PB), Gold and Silver fell apart. The evening performance was even better, about 55 minutes, whereas Robby and PB, Gold and Silver only fell apart at the "scream" EVS sequence and the whole Las Vegas sequence.

But there were times when I got "into" the movie, and almost forgot I was driving.

There is definitely such a thing as LIVE CINEMA, and I know a lot about it now.

The hairy part was when Tony comes into the Silverfish—they sent Chiara too soon; plus the problem that PB is too long, so you can't cut to the specific cues the "dialogue" makes. I suggest three loops: (a) Tony buttons, (b) Chiara buttons, and (c) TV documentary. They can be accessed at any time.

Then the Robby PB can be present in sync with the dialogue.

That—plus my poor editing on:
a) the big Alison/Tony scene
b) the Chiara cooks spaghetti scene
c) and really all the edited sequences (Why not ask Greg to help?)

I'm tired—a great day, a great experience, and a great achievement.

JUNE 4, 2015

This is now Thursday; had I not added the two extra days, this would be the day after the event and thus the press conference.

Here's my warning for the NEXT TWO DAYS:
- HELP ROBBY EDITING PLAYBACK VT (MAKE DATE).
- FIX CHIARA COOKING (HAVE GREG HELP EDITING).
- HAVE 15 MINUTES PLAYING GAMES IN ACTORS ROOM WITH CAST.
- LAS VEGAS SEQUENCE HAS TO BE PINNED DOWN.
- BE SURE I AM OUT OF WAY DURING TONY IN SILVERFISH.
- PRE-FILM FFC WALK, ENDING WITH TAMALES/CHILI CON CARNE & ROYAL CROWN COLA (WITH GLASSES).
- MAKE SPAGHETTI FOR CHIARA—ENOUGH FOR FAMILY.
- LISTEN TO BRIAN'S FAMILY PIANO CUE?
- TELL ALEC (FRANCIE): SLOW DOWN WHILE PULLING TELEGRAM STRIPS—ENUNCIATE.
- ALL ACTION SCENES: GO FOR IT (PERFORMANCE ONLY).
- TELL TERI TO INCLUDE V'S POV OF AX IN WOOD INSERT.
- BE CONSERVATIVE WITH CUTAWAY NICKY'S COMMENTARY.
- WHO SHOULD KEEP AN EYE ON OVERALL COLOR BALANCE AND BRIGHTNESS? MIKE DENNEY?
- CAR SOUND PULL UP: ADD TO VT.
- COLOR SHOTS OF HOLLYWOOD '50s.
- USE SOFIA PINK CELLOPHANE FOR ARCHIE/CHIARA'S DANCING SCENE.
- RECORD MORE CURTAIN CALLS, FOLLOW THROUGH WITH PAT ON STUDIO JIB.

JUNE 5, 2015

PART ONE

(MAKEUP) Darryl has long hair in nostrils.

SWITCHING—Shot waits, takes too long on Tony getting into Silverfish.

ACTION CUT—Go from TONY BUTTONS, to SHOT OF NY, CU TONY to shot of Hollywood back to DARRYL.

On TONY MCU as he explains modern television "no difference—" and then to
TONY BUTTONS as he talks about his grandfather Vincenzo and then
PKG of Robby PB as we see old views of VINCENT.

CU DARRYL—"So the Corrado family was . . . television itself."
CU TONY—"one of the thousands who worked on it, standing. . . ."
CUT TO: ROBBY PB, Vincenzo by the machine.

CUT TO: BACK SHOT - TONY & CHIARA JR, "Tell him about Senza Naso."
CUT TO: DARRYL (leaning forward), "What is Senza Naso?" (as if a scoop).
CU TONY: "Senza Naso is what we call . . ."
MUSIC SOURCE: FADE IN gently, "Caruso recording" setting mood. CUT TO: PHOTO OF SENZA NASO & more photos (before wedding), and we CUT TO CU TONY telling story, says, "best medicine could do."

BACK ANGLE—TONY & CHIARA—Tony prompts Chiara Jr. to tell story: "Married her himself."

ACTION TD CUT—As TONY SAYS, "These are all live feeds." TONY BUTTONS WITH MANY CLIPS (OF DOCU, NY HARLEM PARADE, CHIARA BUTTONS, POV OF MONITORS/IMAGES)—CU TONY.

CU DARRYL: "Is your grandfather. "LF—CU VINCENZO with bowling pins.
CUT TO TONY: "No my father." CUT TO: PHOTO* REAL ARCHIE WITH FLUTE (ON WALL), THEN ARCHIE WAITING WITH MIRROR.

WIDE SHOT "FISH" "Little Chiara's grandmother & namesake" go to: MUSIC UP, ROBBY PB CHIARA typing & V.O. "My name is Chiara. . . ."
MUSIC SOURCE—*Fades up hauntingly.

repeated?

ACTOR—have Darryl wait 6 counts (as Chiara Jr crosses into Silverfish).

(EDIT VT) Possibly tighten Darryl CU for later scenes (when no window).

Pix of (car?) too long.

VT PGK Slower OPTICALS (dissolves, etc) in Italian army story about Rimini.

SOUND Tony's VO too soft when Vin is praying. Hold on ROBBY PB until Mother-in-law Italian style: MUSIC begins "take out from VO "ta da" So can go to piano downbeat on "Style."

STAGING—Chair more to her right while holding flowers, then after door slams, rushes to her new position helping with dishes.

CU FILOMENA: "We don't want any puttane" NEW BRIAN MUSIC on "puttane" parody of whores, & showgirls. (puttane music)

CU Chiara PB ROB VO "Not like my papa's house." cut to Vin entrance.
SCENIC (Brent, can we get an old-fashioned picture to hang above where stove is, without disturbing your ax rig but giving more sense of room when we shoot that direction?)

MUSIC on VINCENZO coming to table (La Boheme theme on piano) then FILO: "We only want a boy." FILO leans in to VIN, "we have enough puttane." TD go shot for slap just before he slaps her. ACTOR: Vin. Make sound with his hand slapping her, close to her face. ACTION TD CUT from SLAP to WILLY SHOT, as he comes into frame: "Mom's right," TD cut to MCS Vin throws bowl at him, "Stupid son I got." cut to Filo (ACTOR: showing bloody mouth to VIN), "Husband pays good" (when Vin punches Filo, "shut up" should short jab at her) to MS as WILLY jumps across table at Vin, cut to Chiara, INSERT PAIL WITH AX, CUT TO: MCS. Vin takes AX, ready to throw, cut to Chiara, Vin throwing ax, CU Archie, them pulling Willy back just as ax goes into wall, cut to VIN furious, cut to Archie getting Willy down to door, C. ACTOR Vin waits two beats before Archie following (a little to his left) with Vin cursing, & slams door, TD waits two beats, on door, then cut to MS as Vin (hooking right to his seat) comes back toward cowering (ACTOR) Filomena, cut to CU Chiara (ACTOR Alex more to his left over Chiara's shoulder), cut to MS as Vin sits down. ACTOR Nick too stiff as Vin raps with his glass (new shot, Insert glass rapping on TD's loop), ACTOR Filo turns her back, thinking "Fill your own glass." cut to CHIARA, she goes to fill it.

Cut to MS Chiara filling glass as Vin goes on about "my seven little wops and La Stampa."
Cut to best Vin Shot for "welcome young lady . . ." starts talking about precision and juggles oranges.

ACTOR—cut too early for Archie to pull curtain (does so while Vin is still juggling). Cut to
Chiara seeing boys out there, pulls curtain while sticking tongue out. MUSIC comes up sensually. Her line about "Papa's house" coming out of boy's spying. CAMERA (C 2 shot) hold, adjusting only subtly. Be on Chiara CU "How will we live if you don't play the flute." Make last jib rise, beautiful and with MUSIC with feeling.

COMMERCIAL BREAK (PART TWO)

ACTOR Archie, be careful that you enter through the Door (wait in place where we don't see you).
CAMERA pre-frame for Chiara popping up "I hope it's a girl." Archie looks up, "a baby."
For shot with scrapbook use tight MS. ACTOR "but as a flute player" not angry, more sadly, defeated "but as a flute player." As IF saying, "yeah, but as a water boy."

TD fast cut to SHOT now tighter CU of Darryl, leaning forward as if to catch a scoop: "What vow?" Fast cut to back angle in "fish" (ACTOR C Jr "A promise to God . . ." etc.) CU Tony, "the vow he made to."

PB ROBBY—Can Italian flag wipe be more feathered? (PB ROBBY—Can Italian image be colored more GOLD?), Can Vin be placed more down in image of Bernalda streets?
*Can real photo of Carmine (on door) be inserted dissolve right after Vin. "Give me a son," as new element of PB ROB. then go on with American montage, SOUND PIANO music with FLUTE segueing back and forth until Carnegie Hall image of FLUTE, and (ARCHIE Flute playing on and gently fading to BLACK. PB - ** John change cut of Chiara cooking the way your original had it with pan first then C' VO and no pre-lap as I had asked for. (new shot ARCHIE's CU SAYING "Just cook same thing each night, etc) bring on "SUNDAY" when Chiara slaps her head (extend that shot 8 frms).

ACTOR—Hold new bowl of spaghetti higher as if a food commercial and you're making sure we see it (higher than waist and tilted so we see how beautiful director made it!). After "stai zito" TD quick cut to CU Archie, then back to Vin testing (Archie in a little closer). ACTOR—Vin says "I know you was a good Neapolitan cook" before all the laughing, or make laughing a little short, then say line, and all are relieved.

TD We should avoid Vincenzo around Archie line "Sit me as far from the bill as possible," cutting around family so VINCENZO CAN LEAVE A PRESET HIMSELF FOR NEXT SCENE. Maybe stay on Chiara, as NICK & ARCHIE, present for next scene, Chiara entering it late with as she's wiping hand with dish towel. (ACTOR VIN trying to lift shirt way up so he shows Chiara his scars!!!!!)

MUSIC—Jazzy source music change to similar mood BRIAN piano one of Carmine's music of era "I'm getting Nowhere Fast with You." RB PB little shorter (shot duration). NEW SHOT for TD loop SEAN (spinning FX ball), TD be on Archie/Chiara dancing into room (PROPS Sofia champagne with pink rolled a little down on neck, in ice bucket already open, two glasses there TD cut to CU of them dancing when you can see their faces there). "Only the finest musi-cians" on C's face when she says "but you don't want to play the flute." Cut right after "maybe we can get his autograph." MUSIC sostenuto begins assertively, PB ROBY right to NBC Bldg.,** shorten and tighten Archie's walk, SOUND heavy echoing FOOTSTEPS in rhythm of music (one-two-one-two-one-two). Cut to ONE-TWO rhythm (when NICKY slowly fades into corner of frame feathered.) Keep on until Toscanini room, then only his VO.* (Anahid, flute's second note bad, replace scale?) Cut to Toscanini a touch later when he turns and writes down notes (composition of frame is weak before this moment). Trim head of Archie with flute after "enough for now" C TO FAST:

DARRYL "What did your family . . ." All filming Tony, CU Tony in her viewfinder, when go to MS Chiara Jr asleep on his lap, use wider shot (ACTOR—pick her up and quickly allow him to kiss her so he can say "Fifty dollars a week" right as you move her out). cut to to DARRYL laughing.
SOUND need ROCKS crashing down Samson & Delilah clip.
PIANO/SOUND, rise up louder for Family music. ACTOR Don't pause after thank you, but come right in with "$320 a week." DOLLY

begins pull-back at same rate as move-in, but when Chiara (say all wife of et) to get into your father's song, so PULL BACK IS FASTER AS SHE SINGS. CAMERA too much head room for pull back! FADE TO BLACK and then fade in logo.

FADE IN COMMERCIAL #2.

PART THREE

FADE OUT COMMERICAL TO BLACK, then LOGO AND PB ROBBY SOUND STREET ACTIVITY, DISTANT SIRENS, SENSE OF WARTIME USA B.G.
ACTOR warden WITH FLASH, wait to be sure she shuts door then hurries off to next house. ACTOR—change manuscript to "symphony." LIGHT lights sweep slowly across their faces as sirens sound, etc., piano emotional.

TD—Be ready for CU Chiara, "Things can happen when you say a Hail Mary." (JIB—FASTER SWING UP TO END.) (PB ROBBY— can we add cars on parkway rather than lights as now, but make the afternoon shots darker.) (ACTOR when Vin drinks water HE CRIES and GROANS, CRYING, not just choking on disgusting water, AS IF it were toilet water) and old man crying like a baby is very disconcerting, Vin, so CRY!!!!! then he thinks of his son playing the flute for Toscanini and this brings great joy to him, his eyes light up and ARCHIE you say the line about getting fired too fast—take a few beats and then it is excruciatingly painful to say.)
CAMEO CU Vin more headroom, and Archie, you're too close to Vin when you say you got fired, you were blocked. FX ROBBY ALL HANDS: Can we make Master Shot with TV? HAVE TV effect (snow) please!!!!! (ARCHIE good: didn't want to disappoint

you. CAMERA, TILT UP MAKE NICE SHOT OF FILO, perhaps a tiny bit closer?

POLIO CONVERSATION, ACTORS, have real conversation back and forth, no one person saying more than 7 beats of time before next person begins their comment. TONY, raise your arm slowly like I showed you I did. ACTOR CUEING: WHEN TONY RAISES ARM SLOWLY is when Chiara ought to lead Vin carrying T slowly across room. when we cut to Master, Archie should walk right through shot carrying Tony, with Chiara watching sadly. ACTORS When they hug and kiss it is out of desperation and love, clinging to each other, then arching slowly goes to pray and Chiara is shocked, he said he'd never get on his knees and pray, but SLOWLY he does, DOLLY SLOWLY MOVE ON HIM, and Fade to black, as typing comes on.* Can "Francis" not be completed before backspaces and begins again with "Tony." ACTORS—START POKER TALK EARLY to help cover for job Set up.

When EVI COMES UP, trim so it can start right on light on Scream. ADD MORE SCREAMS.

When Chiara decides to go for coffee, it is a CHANGE OF PERSONALTY, back to interview, give Chiara a different kind of accent (your own or regional), when she runs into scene WITH HER MORE vehement, really hysterical, Then TD cut to ARCHIE in place as MUSIC crescendos GERSHWIN, ACTOR Chiara gets into pathetic EMBRYO position on chair, quickly so TD can cut to it as if you've been there in that position an hour, exhausted. CAMERA Don't move after you get BEST COMPOSITION ON CHIARA. CHIARA DON'T EXIT, STAY IN YOUR (CAMERA COMPOSITION ON SITTING CHIARA) PLACE ON CHAIR AFTER YOU say you don't want Tony in the house.

PB FFC package, TD should cut straight from Chiara 's line "I don't want him in the house with Lia, CUT TO, Fish door opening!!!!!

PKG re-cut FFC talking about Royal Crown bottles, EDIT SO THAT we cut to Archie sliding onions onto plates while FFC is standing there, then when FFC says wrong bottles, and hand gestures setting the scene, CUT TO MISMATCHED real table with real Royal Crown Bottles.
LINE of Dial. EDIT sound from best take of young FC (ALEX) saying "not coming from me to you but as if I am coming"—he puts emphasis on wrong word in chosen take. (EDIT Push in on chart Tony holds, so it's TIGHER INSERT.)

RUSHING toward Tree (all actors rushing to set up SOUND of jingle type bells) Christmas scene (ACTORS GOOD), BUT handheld camera (CAMERA) should hold no less than 7 counts on each shot, never could get VIN HOLDING EUREKA Sign and looking through microscope.

When Chiara sings Italian song, she should pause and look at Archie (CU Archie, who says "With w—w-w-whom did you study?" Then she breaks out into a robust phrase, SENZA MAMA, and TD we fade on that.
TD—Don't go to colored lights at end; perhaps we could use them earlier, ?? before family and handheld camera all rush in.

COMMERCIAL—WINE AND FILM

SOUND - GIVE faint sound of director (Mike Denney) giving cut instructions and finger snaps (as if this commercial is being made live).

ACTOR—Alison, what you're saying to Tony is that Archie's not ready for his break (not gift) but only, "now," meaning she's encouraging Tony to keep trying. She loves Archie and wants to see Tony succeed in giving him his break. When she goes off, it's to make dinner—have her come on and put black on Tony, about 8 beats later. SWEAT on Archie's BROW.

WHEN WE DO Calendars, DISSOLVE OR IRIS IN SOFT, BRIAN PLAYING PIANO

—TD right after Darryl lifts slate to face (redo?) and snaps it, go to SHOT Alison's CAM FEED.
The ACTOR (TONY Say your line standing by door, and then move to couch repeating "This movie is terrible.") SHOTS Archie by piano, all these shots were better before. NOT AS GOOD, fix Shots.

PG LAS VEGAS, ** add a few cuts of OFTH shots, up street, one or two other quick ones, before establishing SILVERFISH with Vegas chroma.

new INTER FISH scenes instructions ** given.

ACTOR Darryl, Steven, more pandemonium about TIME OF BROADCAST, handing papers to Darryl, Darryl talking to suits, begging, threatening to take his show elsewhere if they don't let show continue, negotiating with suits, maybe even talking to head of CBS: "Les, Les this and Les that."

When FISH DOOR IS OPENED, we must have shots of Teri and others RUSHING in and trying to take command of Fish as if it was an endangered 747, pushing buttons, QUICK cuts of different monitors, warning banner, action AS TD tries to gain control of fish.

Shot EVS of Archie slumped by piano, with his VO about his son's success and big limo TIME extended banner on lower part of frame during limo scene (but out after returns from Telegram scene).

pb DON'T HAVE ARCH CORRADO ON MARQUEE RADIO CITY POV. CUT TO CU TONY IN FISH, WORRYING ABOUT BANNER.

ACTOR—Have Alec young FFC check his telegram last lines with me, intend to cut a few lines. He loves hearing his father happy, but when CHIARA says should pack right away, and he says YES, then Tony realizes how deep he's in and has to say it's a fake.
ALEC say lines slow enough so we understand his words. AFTER WIPE back to Limo, trim heads (pb) so it starts with "I'm sorry" right after wipe back.
PB HARRY CONNICK UNTIL JIB READY, THEN PAT passionately & quickly swing down to Archie conducting. When Tony and Chiara TILT DOWN, Tony—don't take her hand until camera sees that action.
SOUND NICE, segue from song, to sounds of Grammys.

When Archie does win, TAKE OUT blue BORDER so it's just CU. TD Cut to Ambulance, when Chiara is talking to his ear.

AMBULANCE good light show. TD First CU Tony in ambulance, then Archie, cut for scene favoring Archie (ACTORS When laughing, insane laughter, hysterical), then Archie right into "What's happening?" CU Tony, you've had a stroke. After he says line "We always knew you'd be a success," SLOWLY Tony bends to kiss his SWEATY brow and SLOWLY rises UP, take sees his father dead.

CU Archie dead (ACTOR—place your baton higher on shoulder). TONY breaks down for 8 beats, but ends up (TD Cut to MS ambulance, driving away, Tony lying on his dead father's breast) sobbing for his Daddy. SOUND continue these murmurs of Daddy.
ACTOR "Don't go . . . Daddy come back, please don't go, don't leave me without you, I love you so . . . " etc., but when SNOW interrupts, sound of Tony's voice is CUT off with Snow.

JUNE 6, 2015

I'm grateful and I think what with the LA screening and even the NY screening, the concept of LIVE CINEMA is on the map. So this investment did two things really: one was to prove the concept and also get a glimpse of the characters actually functioning in the story, another to have some possible production companies caught up in its excitement and choose to underwrite the next steps.

I am physically tired now, not having slept well for many weeks (?), and so looking forward to NYC and all that waits for me there: Morton St., Snoetta dinner, Sofia and my little granddaughters, Uncle Kiki, the Annette Insdorf lecture to YMCA group—and so on.

Don't have much more to say, but this experience in OKC illustrates how patterns can be created, new friends and colleagues all thrown together over a matter of weeks. Also, how comforting to have the car I wanted waiting for me, the condo comfortable with practical kitchen, exercise setup, and SONOS sound system.

Next time I have to do it I will know how.

JUNE 7, 2015

New York. SHORT DV is over, and seemingly a success. I can relax and enjoy NY. Want to contact that JPM tech guy and make a schedule for the city.

JUNE 9, 2015

Now it's Tuesday, and once again there's too much swimming around in my head. I have a touch concern that I've been in a manic phase now a bit, and so must guard against a depression. How: some meditation (Gracious and Merciful God). Perhaps some turn-off-mind time. However, I know how to do it. Think of nothing, or rather one thing—some activity that requires no brain (sex, cooking, hmmm, need to figure out how to turn off brain).

Regarding Live Cinema, it seems the key is to learn how to build a pre-visualization. I think it has to do with taking a frame, and cramming into it the elements needed, sort of like I did with the Chiara sleeping/Archie telephone call scene. That was manufactured into the "frame," and the logic of where he really was in relation to her was nil. So I could get some "stand-ins" and then use them to cram into "frame" regardless of the logic of the staging, or then stage and build the set to work for those frames, sort of really, Independent Frame. Frame first, then staging, then set?

Maybe Craig Weiss could help me develop that method. Maybe I could set up such a pre-visualization lag in Stage 22? Maybe John Lasseter could advise me.

Dear George,

I just concluded 18 days in Oklahoma City, at a small community college (OCCC), which has a trade-school–type program in film. We made an experimental project as a class I conducted with 74 students—and I took their single sound stage, drove the Silverfish there, and made an experiment in what I call LIVE CINEMA. Live Cinema is a medium which is performed live, but uses the movie-style "shot" as its basis, and not like live TV, which uses the "event" coverage as its basis. Nor is it merely a play (Peter Pan) with a lot of cameras panning around to "cover it." Live TV is always lit from the grid above, with lots of light because they use zoom lenses to avoid seeing the camera, which are notoriously slow.

I used half-and-half flat lenses with some quality zooms, lit from the floor (rolling LED battery-powered lights) and made more movie-style—yet the whole piece was performed live, including the music score.

Everyone, including actors, were local from Oklahoma City, aside from me and my team from Napa, a local theater stage manager, and about three TV professionals to help the students, who were all kids from my class and got college credits. All is LIVE other than obvious stock footage. Weird arty cutting was done live with the help of those EVS machines that are used in football game replays. Over the concluding CREDITS you see a high view of the stage, which is amazingly empty and sparse: a few chairs, a mattress, some tables and a door and window. My personal assignment was to see how all the stuff developed for modern television (sports) could be applied to storytelling. I hope I have piqued your interest, dear

George—you know me, always jumping over cliffs! which this experience certainly was: it was seen live in five theaters with small audiences of colleagues and friends: Paris, NYC, LA, SF, and NAPA.

If your home screening room has connection to internet (Apple TV or computer), which I'm sure it does, you can see it there. It's a bit shabby, with some mistakes, but what the hell!

AFTERTHOUGHT

I confess I've been curious how practitioners or "cinemawrights" (movie makers) could get in on the ludicrous art market where a piece of "something" could be valued at tens if not hundreds of millions of dollars and offered by a gallery, as this would need be something one could "own," not withstanding Matthew Barney's good fortune of selling his five *Cremaster* movie DVD sets for over $100,000 per set. A thought that popped into my mind was this: create a "box" that would sell for extraordinary amounts in limited edition. This box would be numbered and signed and contain a sealed hard drive, and would connect to the internet in a way that would enable it to receive a live-streamed broadcast of an original cinematic work. Only these few boxes would receive the live performance, and it could not be reproduced. Its only function is that it could be owned (and thus sold) and screened as often as wished, for its owner and guests, paralleling an owned painting or other work of art.

GLOSSARY

analog An electrical signal that continuously varies as it records where the output is proportional to the input.

Appia effect Developed by Adolphe Appia (1862–1928) a Swiss theatrical designer and writer, an Appia effect is a stage lighting effect that uses shadow against light to create depth between performers and the stage.

associate director (AD) The AD assists the director with major creative decisions and helps with the camera setups and shot selection.

backlot An outdoor space on a movie studio lot where sets are built and used for exterior shots.

bandwidth A range of frequencies used to transmit electronic signals.

cathode ray tube (CRT) A focused beam of electrons used to display images on a screen by use of a vacuum tube.

chroma key The method of using blue or green screens as backdrops so that the given color can be isolated and removed from the video signal in order to add special effects in post-production.

coverage Every individual shot for a particular scene, which the editor will use to assemble the final cut.

crew A group of film technicians and other behind-the-camera individuals involved in the making of a production.

dailies The best takes from a day's shooting, typically viewed the following day and used to check the quality of the footage.

director of photography (DP) The DP oversees the overall image of the picture, including lighting and framing the compositions of the shots, and ensuring an even balance between them.

dolly A mobile platform that typically carries the camera and its operator to allow for smooth moving shots, sometimes rolling on tracks or a level floor and pushed by a crew member.

dress rehearsal A full-scale and final rehearsal before a live performance in which the actors are fully dressed in wardrobe and makeup.

EVS replay server A machine used in live video broadcast productions that enables the instant playback of edited audio and video feeds.

foley Commonplace synchronized sound effects added to a film in post-production.

4K and 8K cameras The resolution of digital television and cinematography; 8K is currently the highest frame size with regard to horizontal pixel count, while 4K is the current standard.

frame rate The rate per second at which a shutter opens and closes, capturing images called frames.

frame rate converter A device used to change the frame rate, often used to match mismatched frame rates between cameras/equipment.

gaffer The chief electrician responsible for the lighting of the production, who takes direction from the DP.

genlock Short for "generator locking," can be achieved by using a common reference signal to synchronize multiple video sources.

handheld A technique utilized by camera operators to handhold a camera during shooting rather than mount it to a tripod/base.

helical scan tape recorder A magnetic tape recorder used to record high-frequency signals.

IP control Short for Internet Protocol, IP control is a web-based interface that allows electronic devices to be controlled over a network.

Kinescope The recording of a television production through the lens of a film camera situated directly in front of the monitor or television screen. At one time, this was the only method for recording and preserving live television.

master shot The single, continuous shot encompassing an entire scene from start to finish, oftentimes a long shot that will later be intercut with middle shots and close-ups.

matrix board A piece of equipment that allows multiple input signals to be routed to a variety of outputs.

mixing board A device with multiple audio inputs used to adjust levels and equalize and affect each audio input signal, primarily used to create a "mixdown" of all available audio signals.

montage An assembly of footage edited and pieced together to produce a consistent, fluid sequence.

motion control An electronically programmed camera system with repeatable movements, often used to capture different elements of a scene with the same camera movement so that they can be more easily composited into a single special effects shot.

multiviewer A single display capable of showing multiple video sources, often in a grid pattern (2x2, 3x3, 4x4, etc.).

nonlinear editing The temporary digital editing of a video production that can be used for live television but does not permanently alter the source material.

practical Any normal functioning part of the set that does not need to be hidden from the camera, such as a visible desk lamp providing the light for the scene.

pre-visualization The method of foreseeing an entire scene or complete work, shot by shot, by use of physical materials such as storyboards and sound recordings.

prime (flat) lens A camera lens with a fixed focal length. Although less versatile than a zoom, prime lenses often provide superior optical quality and wider apertures.

rear projection The projection of a pre-filmed still or moving picture set against the backdrop so that the live action and background can be filmed as a single image.

run-through A full-scale rehearsal that is not filmed.

scenic panel Movable panels used for background scenic walls/ decorations.

second unit A team of film technicians responsible for additional footage not requiring the principal actors.

snoot An attachment used on lighting fixtures to restrict illumination and prevent glare.

Steadicam A device often comprised of an arm, vest, and sled that enables the operator to stabilize the camera during handheld shots, ensuring smooth movement.

storyboard A representation of a scene, shot by shot, through the use of drawings that provide a clear and concise visual plan for production.

sync Short for synchronization, sync refers to properly lining up sound with the picture.

tally light A small signal light attached to the front of a camera to notify actors and crew when that camera is live.

technical director (TD) The TD is responsible for the operations of the video mixing panel and for ensuring that all members of the crew are ready and in place prior to broadcast.

Translight An illuminated film backing used as a backdrop so that issues such as weather and time of day do not impede production.

video mixing panel A control surface with a multitude of buttons and "t-handles" that communicates directly with the video switcher, used by the TD to choose between camera feeds during the production.

video switcher A device with multiple video inputs that allows the switching between the video sources, creating a single picture as seen by the audience or viewer.

zoom lens A camera lens with a variable focal length that allows the shot to move toward or away from its subject while the camera itself remains stationary.

CREDITS OF THE LIVE BROADCASTS

Distant Vision
presented by Live Cinema LLC
in association with Oklahoma City Community College
Oklahoma City, OK

BROADCAST LIVE ON JUNE 5, 2015

Written and Directed by	Francis Ford Coppola
Producer	Jenny Gersten
Executive Producer	Anahid Nazarian
Technical Producer	Masa Tsuyuki
Consulting Producer	Gray Frederickson
Stage Manager	Steve Emerson
First Assistant Stage Manager	Daniel Leeman Smith

Second Assistant Stage Manager	Corey Morgan
Director of Photography	Mihai Malaimare, Jr.
Composer	Brian W. Tidwell
Editor	Robert Schafer
Technical Director	Teri Rozic
Associate Director	Wendy Garrett
Television Consultant	Mike Denney
Camera Technical Supervisor	Stacy Mize
Directing Consultant	Owen Renfroe
Costumes	Lloyd Cracknell
Costume Associates	Kelsey Godfrey Christopher Harris Tiffany Keith Jessie Mahon
Hair/Wigs/Makeup	Steven Bryant
Sound Director	Kini Kay
Sound Mixer	James Russell

Mic Czar	Grant Provence
QLab Czar	Eli Mapes
Key Gaffer	Sean Lynch
Prop Master	Peggy Hoshall
Scenic Director	Brent Noel
Wardrobe Supervisor	Jenava Burguriere
Fight Director	Tom Huston Orr
Director, Film and Video Department	Greg Mellott

CAST (*IN ORDER OF APPEARANCE*)

Darryl	Darryl Cox
Tony	Brady McInnes
Alison	Jennifer Laine Williams
Young Chiara/Lia	Nani Barton
Passersby	Mark Fairchild
	Daraja Stewart

Policeman	Patrick Martino
Willy/Boy on Bike	Hayden Marino
Chiara	Chandler Ryan
Filomena	Thesa Loving
Archie	Jeffrey Schmidt
Nicky	Colin Morrow
Young Tony	Alex Irwin
Shadow Girl	Kelsey Godfrey
Vincenzo	Mike Kimmel
Midwife/Poker Player	Miranda LoPresti
Young Filomena	Anna Miller
Toscanini	Aidino Cassar
Warden	Stephen Morrow
Charlotte	Cait Brasel
RCMH Musicians	Lemuel Bardeguez Richard Charnay Brian W. Tidwell

Flutist	Anahid Nazarian
Pianist	Brian W. Tidwell
Camera Operators	Reese Baker
	Alejandro Carreno
	Mitch R. Cruse
	Johnathon Cunningham
	Fransua Durazo
	Pat Flanagan
	Sarah Hoch
	Jason Hyman
	Lanchi Le
	Cray McDaniel
	Stacy Mize
	Scott Morris
	John Nation
	Sunday Omopariola
	Sam Pemberton
	Jim Ritchey
	David Santos
	Clay Taylor
	Ryan Rockwell Thomas
	Haden Tolbert
	Carlos Torres
	Agnes Wright
Grip	Ford Austin
Technical Assistant	Brandon Wakely

Production Crew	LaShawna Collins
	Tyler Frederickson
	Terry Joiner
	Karen Martinez
	Stephen Morrow
	Taylor Tyree
Subrouter Technical Director	Eugene Ticzon, Jr.
3Play Operators	Grant Horoho
	Zachary West
VT AD	Joshua L. Buzzard
	Ron Huff
	Lizeth Melendez
	Keegan Parrish
Video Operator	Troy Braghini
Tech Manager Assistant	Noble Banks
Stage Management Crew	Logan Conyers
	Pedro Ivo Diniz
	Nichole Harwell
	Nathan Larrinaga II
	Landon Morgan
	Joseph Mwangi

Sound Crew	Derek Biggers
	Lauren Bumgarner
	Rhett Chanley
	Charles K. Golden
	Colby Kopel
Grip & Electric Crew	Paul T. Chambers
	Ken Cole
	Whitson Crynes
	C. S. Giles
	Shae Rody Orcutt
	Keith Eric Parks
	Brooke Shackleford
Art Department	Bailey Hartman
	Isaac Herrera
	Nathan Larrinaga
	Josef McGee
	Quinton Mountain
	Kathy Do Nguyen
Documentary Crew	Cait Brasel
	Jonathan Shahan
Additional Documentary Filming	Ford Austin
	Agnes Wright
Director's Assistant	Rachel Petillo

Actor Handlers   Roman Alcantara
Cheyenne Clawson
Mark Fairchild
Miranda LoPresti
Anna Miller
Taylor Reich
Tiffane Shorter
Daraja Stewart

Second Unit/NYC

Director of Photography   Rob Brink

Driver   Gerard Dervan

Special Thanks:
Major League Baseball
Corey Parker and Brady Belavek, VER
Mike Denney
EMSA, John Graham
Annette Insdorf
Tom Kaplan
Tom Huston Orr
Oklahoma University Theater Department
Oklahoma City Repertory Theatre
Cathy from OCCC IT
Randy Hodge
The Rink Gallery

Very Special Thanks:
Ruth Charnay Dean of Arts
Oklahoma City Community College
and the entire Oklahoma City Community
College Staff, Faculty and Facilities Crew

Filmed live entirely at the Visual and Performing Arts Center
of Oklahoma City Community College

Our warmest thanks to the kind and hospitable people
of Oklahoma

Distant Vision
presented by Live Cinema LLC
in association with the UCLA School of Theater,
Film and Television
Los Angeles, CA

BROADCAST LIVE ON JULY 22, 2016

Written and Directed by	Francis Ford Coppola
Producer	Jenny Gersten
Executive Producer	Anahid Nazarian
Line Producer	Adriana Rotaru
Technical Producer	Masa Tsuyuki
Director of Photography	Mihai Malaimare, Jr.
Scenic and Production Designer	Sydnie Ponic
Gaffer and Lighting Designer	Pablo Santiago
Costume Designer	Ruoxuan Li
Composer	Brian W. Tidwell
Editor	Robert Schafer

Technical Director	Teri Rozic
Broadcast Technical Supervisor	David Crivelli
Production Stage Manager	Lee Micklin
Stage Manager	Kellie D. Knight
Casting	Courtney Bright Nicole Daniels
Associate Director	Chris Ellner
Production Supervisor	Gretchen Landau

For the UCLA School of Theater, Film and Television:

Producer	Jeff Burke
Director of Production, Theater	Daniel Ionazzi
Production Manager	Jeff Wachtel
Assistant Producer	Reina Higashitani
Dean	Teri Schwartz

Faculty Advisors Kathleen McHugh, Chair,
Film, Television and Digital
Media
Brian Kite, Chair, Theater
J. Ed Araiza
Jeff Burke
Myung Hee Cho
Tom Denove
Kristy Guevara-Flanagan
Michael Hackett
Deborah Landis
Jane Ruhm
Becky Smith

CAST (*IN ORDER OF APPEARANCE*)

Young Tony Alexander Niles

Richie/Danny Ethan DiSalvio

Chiara Lea Madda

TV Interviewer Beth Lane

Tony Israel Lopez Reyes

Alison Marguerite French

Young Chiara Ella Giufre

Policeman	Beck DeRobertis
Zopo	Freddie Donelli
Alfonso	Lou Volpe
Z'Ciccillo	Roberto Bonanni
Pizzutti	Luca Guastini
Osualdo	Luca Della Valle
Agostino	Mario Di Donato
Star Boarder	Nicola Gaballo
Filomena	Francesca Fanti
Mr. Miller	Skip Pipo
Archie	Matteo Voth
Nicky	Salomon Tawil
Willy	Kaden Rizzo
Miriam	Remi Deupree
Mrs. Miller	Fannie Brett
Z'Antoinetta	Paola Perla Cufaro

La Marescialla	LizBeth Lucca
Alexander Graham Bell	Bertrand-Xavier Corbi
Watson	John Dellaporta
French Scientist	Franck Amiach
Jenkins Broadcast Performers	Haley Camille
	Ellen Durnal
	Jace Febo
	Marguerite French
	Sionne Elise Tollefsrud
	Ella Giufre
	Skip Pipo
Doctor	David Landau
Z'Peppine	Carlo Carere
Z'Carolina	Cristina Lizzul
Bino	Andrew Coulan
Donnie	Brian Coulan
Ignazio	Jace Febo
Italian Tough Kid	Jentzen Ramirez
Jewish Newsboy	Jesse James Baldwin

Ice Man	Giuseppe Russo
Antonio	Luca Riemma
Band Members	Oscar Emmanuel Fabela
	Alex Parmentier
Stunt Doubles	Sergei Smitriev
	Joe Sobalo, Jr.

Neighbors and Partygoers:

Children	Willow Beauoy
	Bailey Bucher
	Haley Camille
	Samantha Desman
	Samantha Hamilton
	Trinity Lee
	Giana Lendzion
	Nico Lendzion
	Juliana Sada

Women	Laura Fantuzzi
	Roberta Geremicca
	Cristina Lippolis
	Francesca de Luca
	Tatiana Luter
	Ada Mauro
	Davia Schendel
	Christine Uhebe
	Arianna Veronesi

Men	Will Block
	James Distefano
	Samuel Kay
	Gianluca Malacrino
	Gianfranco Terrin
Casting PA	Erica Silverman
Movement Coordinator	Angela Lopez
Assistant Stage Managers	Amani Alsaied
	Patrick Hurley
Understudies/Actor Assistants	Camryn Burton
	Alex Parmentier
	Davia Schendel
	Masaya Tajika
Musicians	Brian W. Tidwell, piano
	Thomas Feng, keyboard/ synthesizer
	Alexandru Malaimare, violin
	Isaac Enciso, flute
Assistant to Director of Photography	Marcus Patterson
Technical Director for Camera	Mark Daniel Quintos
Camera Production Coordinator	Scott Barnhardt

Camera	Hanxiong Bo
	Michael Bromberg
	Marcus C.W. Chan
	John Dellaporta
	Jackson DeLoach
	Julia Ponce Diaz
	Kathryn Elise Drexler
	Oscar Emmanuel Fabela
	Peter Fuller
	Anthony Giacomelli
	Alicia Herder
	Gwendolyn Infusino
	Silvia Lara
	Mads Larsen
	Kevin Lee
	Lia Lenart
	Christine Liang
	Andrew St. Maurice
	Emily Rose Mikolitch
	Nathaniel Nguyen-Le
	Marta Savina
	Meedo Taha
	Sionne Elise Tollefsrud
	Tara Turnbull
	Siru Wen
	Ying Yan
EVS operators	Chris Ybarra
	Alex Williams
	Michael Wilson
	Ruben Corona

IP Director Operator/ EVS Operator	Amy Khuong
DIT	Eli Berg
Assistant to Technical Producer	Kelly Urban
Assistant Editor	John Cerrito
Art Director & Set Decorator	Hogan Lee
Assistant Set Designer/ Wall Czar	James Maloof
Video Projection Designer	Zach Titterington
Prop Master	Liz Sherrier
Set Decorator	Tatiana Kuilanoff
Props on Set/Wall Movers	Alexander De Koning Amber Li Matthew McLaughlin Jay Shipman
Art Department Assistants	Irena Ajic Michelle Joo Samantha Vinzon
Costume Supervisor	Kumie Asai

Faculty Costume Advisor	Jane Ruhm
Key Costumers	Chanèle Casaubon
	Phoebe Longhi
	Lia Wallfish
Set Costumers	Brian Carrera
	Chad Mata
	Keelin Quigley
	Kelsey Smith
Stitchers	Richard Turk Magnanti
	Minta Manning
Key Makeup Artist	Valli O'Reilly
Key Hair Stylist	Barbara Lorenz
Hair Stylists	Steven Soussana
	Kristin Arrigo
	Sapphire Harris
	Marie Larkin
	Norma Lee
	Anissa Salazar
Makeup Artists	Leslie Devlin
	Stephanie McCuskey
	Viola Rock
	Becky Swasen

Master Electricians	Phill Powers
	Alif Marchi
Board Operator	Austin Burkett
Best Boy Electric	Lesley Elizondo
Electrician	Adamma Ebo
	Kadriya Gizatullina
	Stephen Heleker
Key Grip	Justin Richards
Best Boy Grip	Pratik Shah
Grip	Eric Glawe
	Brynna Mason
	Jasmine Rodriguez
	Khana Tillman
Sound Supervisor	Jonathan Burke
Sound Mixer	Michael Cooper
Sound System Technician	Jesse Kious
Assistant to Mixer, Playback	Mitch Bradford
Lavalier Crew	Lauren Buangan
	Renee Torchio MacDonald

Boom Crew	Andrew Arnold
	Ezra Sky Peterson Behnen
	Hunter Milano
Intercom Assistant	Ellen Durnal
Production Manager	Kevin Otte
Assistant Production Manager	Lila Ahronowitz
Production Coordinator	Beck DeRobertis
Assistant to Mr. Coppola	Rachel Petillo
Assistant to Technical Producer	John Gittens
Intern to Producers	Leigh Engel
Studio Teachers	Paul Salow
	Dan Benjamin
	Wendy Herron
Nurse	Linda Hoag
Catering	Nick Lorenz
Stunt Coordinator	Pat Romano
Riggers	Duane Burkhart
	Brett Praed
	Brett Sheerin

Stunt Design	Buddy Joe Hooker
Stunt Doubles	Sergei Dmitriev
	Joe Sobalo Jr
Animals	Gods Creatures Grooming
Goat Handlers	Elizabeth Byers
	Ashley Shrader
	Kerry Byers
	Goats: Blaze and Checkers
Liz Flush—Dog Handler	Dog: Popcorn
	Karin Graziani
	(Popcorn's owner)
Skye Swan—Cat Handler	Tiki: the coolest, calmest cat in town
	Stage dog: Gus
Automobile provided by Jay Leno's Garage	Jay Leno
	Steve Reich
	Samantha Reich

Video systems by SVP

Account Manager	Hank Moore
Lead Video Engineer	Spud Murphy
Video Engineer	Lance Cody
	Stephen Sharpe

Utility	John McGregor
	Joey Miranda
	John Dava
	Joey Dibenedetto
	Jeff Broadway
	Chris Thorne
Driver	Tim Huffaker

Streaming Services by Major League Baseball:

MLBAM Remote	James Johnson
	Mark Elinson
	Elliot Weiss
	Jeffrey Milnes
MLBAM New York	Roger Williams
	Greg Bryne
	Aashish Shah
	Raymond Bridgelall
Transmission Services	MX 1
	PSSI Global Services
Communications by VER	Brady Belavek
	Alex Cordova
	Steve Culp
	Jonathan Hogstran
	EVS Technical Manager
	Avi Gonshor
EVS DYVI Specialist	Jurgen Obstfelder

Switcher and replay servers provided by EVS.

Digital cinema cameras provided by Canon U.S.A., Inc.

Video switching in the Silverfish, signal conversion, and additional cameras by Blackmagic Design.

Additional lighting supplied by ARRI and Maccam.

Additional camera support equipment provided by Vitec Group and VER.

Period costumes supplied by Palace Costumes, Western Costume Company, and the UCLA Costume Shop.

Dolly supplied by JL Fisher.

UCLA TFT Shops	Grip & Electric Shop
	Mique Hwang
	Erik Kjonaas
Camera & Equipment Supervisor	Albert Malvaez
Scene Shop Supervisor	Don Dyke
Scene Shop Staff	Michael Sellers
	Ernest Stifel
	Kenneth Houston
	Joe A Lopez

Prop Shop Supervisor	Kevin Williams
Costume Shop Supervisor	Stephanie Workman
Theater Operations Manager	Bridget Kelly
Sound Stage Manager	Rand Soares
IT Support	Fabio Ibarra

Documentary:

Producer	Gayatri Bajpal
Director	Ceci Albertini
Director of Photography	Golden Zhao
Sound & Assistant Editor	Stefan Wanigatunga
Editor and DIT	Thanos Papastergiou

For American Zoetrope:

| Chief Financial Officer | Gordon Wang |
| Executive Administrative Assistant | Nancy DeMerritt |

UCLA TFT and Francis Ford Coppola would like to acknowledge the generosity of **LG Electronics USA** for their generous support of this experimental workshop

Special Thanks:
Milena Canonero
Barry Zegel
Lori Lai
James Mockoski
Gordon Wang
Nancy DeMerritt
Courtney Garcia
Renee Berry
Buddy Joe Hooker
Diana Lendzion
Fred Roos
David Pinkel
Neil Mazzella and Hudson Scenic
Cynthia Rodriguez, YOLA Expo

Very Special Thanks:
Dean Teri Schwartz
Jeff Burke
Reina Higashitani
Kellie Knight
Jeff Wachtel

Filmed live entirely at the UCLA School of Theater, Film and Television

ACKNOWLEDGMENTS

Eleanor Coppola

Anahid Nazarian

Jenny Gersten

Gray Frederickson

Masa Tsuyuki

Teri Rozic

Robert Schafer

Courtney Garcia

Eugene Lee

Peter Baran

Courtney Bright

Nicole Daniels

James Mockoski

Barry Zegel

Robert Weil

INDEX

Page numbers in *italics* refer to illustrations.

Abbey Theatre, 55–57
abstract sets, 55
Academy Awards, 26–27, 70
acetate recording machines, 1, 161
acting, actors:
    contract, 74
    film, 13, 29, 33–34, 38, 42, 61, 70,
        163
    in Live Cinema, xiii, 5–6, 7, 16, 29,
        33–42, 50–51, 86, 92, 93, 95–101,
        104, 105, 125, 126, 129, 134–35, 136,
        137, 139, 140, 144, 146, 150, 151,
        152, 154, 160
    marks for, 99–101
    placement of, 11
    rehearsals, 29, 33–42, 50–51, 55,
        92–99, 129, 132–39, 141, 160, 163
    repertory, 5–6
    self-confidence of, 35–36
    theater, 3, 5–6, 10, 34
action films, 54, 84
action shots, 88–91
Actors Room, 34, 39, 41
adapters, lens, 44
Airstream trailers, 66–68, 67
Allah, 104
Allied Artists, 2
American Graffiti, 70
Amnesia, 14–15

Ampex video recorders, 25
analog signals, 159
Andermann, Andrea, 29, 111
Anderson, Wes, 107
animals, 94, 95, 99
animated films, 11, 12, 51
Antonioni, Michelangelo, 113
apertures, 162
Apocalypse Now, 8, 9, 36–37, 68, 69–70,
    71, 72, 74, 77, 115
Appia, Adolphe, 55, 59, 159
Apple, 74, 157
apprentices, 74
Archer, William, 32
archival copies, 118
arc lights, 111
Arriflex cameras, 107
art, 15, 109, 157
ASC cinematographer's manual, 43
asides, 83
associate directors (ADs), 92–93, 95, 101–
    2, 138, 159
Astaire, Fred, 62
AT&T, 20, 21
Attenborough, Richard, 12
audiences:
    for cinema, xii, 9, 30, 31,
        69–70, 88–91
    for Live Cinema, 7, 16, 30

audiences (*continued*)
    television, 105
    theatrical, 9–10, 30–31
Austin, Tex., 5
auteurs, xii, 27–28
A.V. Club, 79
Avengers, The, 123
awards ceremonies, 104

babies, 94, 104
backdrops, 46, 54, 55, 61, 85, 98, 132,
    159–60, 162
backlots, 61, 159
Baird, John Logie, 22
Baker, George Pierce, 31
Bancroft Junior High, 73
bandwidth, 159
Barney, Matthew, 157
baseball games, 16, 17, 50
basic units, 7–9, 10, 87
battery-powered lights, 52, 54, 55, 98,
    156
Beauty and the Beast, 79
Beggs, Richard, 70*n*
behavior, 7
Bell, Alexander Graham, 18, 19
Berger, Mark, 70*n*
Bergman, Ingmar, 110, 113
Bergman, Ingrid, 25
Berlin, 21–22
Bernstein, Armyan, 71, 72, 73
Bertolucci, Bernardo, 76
"Best Director" Academy Award, 26–27
Best Years of Our Lives, The, 114
Bidwell, Shelford, 18–19
bildungsroman, 117
Birdman, 29
Birth of a Nation, The, 31
Bizet, Georges, 30
black and white films, 113
black cards, 16–17
black curtains, 51–52
Blackmagic, 107
Blackmagic Micro Studio digital
    cameras, 44
Blackmagic Studio digital cameras, 44
Blackmagic Teranex Express frame rate
    converters, 44
blocking, 130

Blow-Up, 114
Bolex 16mm lenses, 44
booms, sound, 136–37
Borgnine, Ernest, 2
Boulanger, Nadia, 126
boxed sets, 157
Boxer, Nathan, 70*n*
Bram Stoker's Dracula, 80
Brando, Marlon, 36–37, 38, 70
Breaking Bad, 26, 28
broadcasts, 1–2, 25, 49, 103–7, 152
Broadway, 23, 24, 30–31
Brown, Garrett, 111
Brown, Jerry, 63–68
Brynner, Yul, 24
Buddenbrooks (Mann), 116–17
Bulow, Hans von, 29–30
Bwana Devil, 109

Caan, James, 38
Cabiria, 31
Caesar, Sid, 28
Camelot, 62
cameras:
    angles and views from, 65–66, 99,
        111, 129, 130
    apertures of, 162
    Arriflex, 107
    classic style for, 84–85
    coordination of, 92–97, 137
    digital, xii, 43, 74, 107–8, 112, 160
    8K, 14–15, 160
    focal lengths of, 162, 164
    4K, 60, 107, 160
    frame rate for, 43–44, 93, 147, 161
    handheld, 54, 84–85, 161, 163
    hand offs of, 85
    Handycam, 108
    lenses for, *see* lenses
    lighting levels and, 76
    live, 6, 95–99, 135–36
    in Live Cinema, 14, 15, 17, 43–44,
        92–97, 110–11, 135
    motion control for, 64, 162
    mounted cards for, 93
    movement of, 7, 8, 54, 55, 84–85
    multiple, 12, 14, 60, 65–66, 76, 92–93,
        111, 135–36, 163–64
    operators of, 65–66, 101, 129, 138

placement of (setups), 29, 86, 99, 130, 131, 139–40, 159
shutters of, 161
single setup for, 29
60i (59.94 interlaced fields per second), 43, 44
stationary, 54
Steadicam, 85, 110–11, 163
style of, 84–85
tally lights for, 93, 163
technology of, 14–15, 21, 43, 44, 60, 107, 160
television, 43, 75, 93
30p (standard TV frame rate), 93
tilting of, 111, 149–50
tripods for, 161
24p (23.98 progressive frames per second), 43–44
video, 106–7, 110
viewfinders for, 75, 129
visibility of, 14, 15
Campbell-Swinton, A. A., 19
Candid Camera, 105
Canon, 107
Canon EOS C300 digital cameras, 44
Captain Video and His Video Rangers, 2
Carmen (Bizet), 30
Carnegie Hall, 147
cartoons, 110
Caruso, Enrico, 143
cathode ray tube (CRT), 19, 21, 159
Cazale, John, 38
CBS, 24, 53, 106–7, 118
CBS Television City, 53, 107, 118
celebrities, 33, 116
celluloid film, xi–xii, 107–8, 109
Century City, 61–62
Cervantes, Miguel de, 123
chairs, 34–35, 41, 129, 133, 145, 150
Channel 5, 2
Channel 13, 2
characterization, 7, 34, 36–42
Chayefsky, Paddy, 2, 24
children, 41, 94, 95, 99, 104
Children's Hour, The, 2
Chinatown, 28
choreography, 99
choruses, 83
chroma key, 46, 54, 64, 66, 85, 159–60

Cimino, Michael, 27
Cinedome Theater, 77
cinema:
    acting in, 13, 29, 33–34, 38, 42, 61, 70, 163
    audiences for, xii, 9, 30, 31, 69–70, 88–91
    auteurs in, xii, 27–28
    basic unit in, 7–9, 10, 87
    classic or traditional, xi–xiii, 3, 7, 15–16, 44, 61–62, 84–85, 87, 99, 103, 105, 112–14
    dailies in, 47, 160
    design in, 84–85
    development of, xi–xii, xiii, 21–22, 61–62, 84–85
    as electronic-digital medium, xi–xii, 3, 14–15, 24, 29–30, 33–34, 107–8
    emotional impact of, 9, 10, 50, 88–91
    essence of, xii, 3, 9–12, 20, 87–91
    exhibition in, 111–12
    expressionism in, 84, 85
    failure in, 62–72
    final cuts in, 160
    formulas in, 83
    genres in, 48, 84
    German, 21–22
    glossary of, 159–64
    Golden Age of, 61–62
    grammar and syntax of, 9–12, 87–91
    history of, 21–22
    industry for, 20, 106
    Japanese, 8
    lighting in, 13, 52, 58–59, 76, 160
    literary adaptations for, 23–24
    Live Cinema compared with, 48, 85–86, 99, 103, 105, 111–12, 118
    masterpieces of, 112–14
    microphones in, 21, 136–37, 138
    montage in, 7, 9, 21, 87–91, 162
    as "moving pictures," 20
    narrative in, 113
    as photochemical-mechanical medium, xi–xii, 107–8, 109
    plays used in, 113
    post-production in, 159–60
    production of, 5, 12, 21, 33, 76, 159–60, 163
    props for, 11–12

cinema (*continued*)
　realism in, 81–86
　rehearsals for, 38, 42
　scenes in, 162
　scripts (screenplays) for, 33–34, 42, 71,
　　72, 75, 99
　sets in, 61–62, 76, 87, 138, 162
　shots in, 2–3, 13–14, 102
　soundstages for, 61–62
　stars in, 33
　start-and-stop, 85
　storytelling in, 21
　style of, 2–3, 8–9, 12, 13, 20, 24, 25,
　　44, 48, 81–91
　television compared with, 2–3, 12, 23,
　　24–28, 78, 112
　theater compared with, 31–32, 83, 84
　see also film, films
Cinema Paradiso, 111
cinematography, 8–9, 70n, 76, 160, 161
"cinemawrights," 157
Citizen Kane, 84
City Magazine, 71
Clark, Petula, 62
classical music, 1, 29–31, 68, 113, 114, 148
classic cinema, xi–xiii, 3, 7, 15–16,
　　44, 61–62, 84–85, 87, 99, 103,
　　105, 112–14)
clichés, 7
close-up (CU) shots, 10, 14, 15, 21, 32,
　　52–53, 60, 88–89, 133, 146–47,
　　153–54, 161
C-mounts, 44
CNN, 26, 85
Coca, Imogene, 28
Coe, Fred, 23
Cold War, 116
color balance, 109, 142
color film, 113
color theory, 108, 109
Comedian, The, 24, 25, 107
comedies, 28–29, 70–71
comedy series, 28–29
commentators, 85
commercials, 20, 132, 146, 149, 151
common reference signals, 161
communication revolution, 27
composers, 29–30
compositing, 86

computers:
　for cameras, 44
　development of, 27, 73–74
　editing on, 74, 110, 162
　mixing with, 45, 98
　scenics generated by, 54
　technology of, 44, 46, 112, 157
"concentration" exercises, 35, 40–41
conductors, music, 1, 29–30
confetti, 101
Conformista, Il, 76
Connick, Harry, Jr., 153
continuity, 85, 135–36
contract actors, 74
Conversation, The, 70
Coppola, August Floyd, 63
Coppola, Carmine, 1, 25, 126, 147
Coppola, Eleanor, 77, 135
Coppola, Francis Ford, 119
　Academy Awards presentation of
　　(1979), 26–27
　Bricktown apartment of, 121–22, 124
　Brown's campaign filmed by, 63–68
　in Buenos Aires, 38–39
　in Cambridge, Mass., 108–10
　Chapter 11 bankruptcy of, 77
　childhood of, 1, 25
　as director, 3, 15–17, 34, 36, 42,
　　63–77, 84, 119
　education of, 73, 75
　Edwin Land met by, 108–10
　family of, 108, 117–18, 125, 131, 135
　finances of, 70–71, 77
　journal of, xiii, 121–57
　Live Cinema developed by, xii–xiii, 1–3,
　　15–17, 27, 34, 76, 77, 84, 115–18, 121–57
　in Los Angeles, 121, 154
　in Madison, Wis., 63–68
　as magazine publisher, 71
　meditation practiced by, 155
　name of, 63
　in New York, 154, 155
　in Oklahoma City, 121–57
　polio of, 2, 150
　as producer, 78–79
　reviews of films by, 69–70, 77, 79–80
　in San Francisco, 71–73
　screenplays by, 3, 71; *see also Dark Elec-
　　tric Vision* (Coppola)

"story and character" notes of, 7–8
television programs watched by, 2–3, 25
as UCLA student, 75
winery owned by, 122
Coppola, Gian-Carlo (Gio), 84, 108
Coppola, Sofia, xii, 8, 9, 107, 154
countdowns, 92
Count of Monte Cristo, The
(Dumas), 82–83, 82
courtroom dramas, 10, 48
coverage, 10, 11, 12–13, 15, 48, 60, 91,
133, 156, 160
Covered Wagon, The, 87
Coward, Noël, 118
cowboy movies, 2, 71
Cracknell, Lloyd, 122–23
Craig, Edward Gordon, 32, 55–59,
56, 86–87, 98
Cremaster series, 157
crews, 17, 93, 95–97, 99, *119*, 135, 160, 163
crisis moments, 16
criticism, 33–34, 69–70, 77, 79–80
Cruze, James, 88
cues, lighting, 92, 132
cues, sound, 137, 138, 141, 142
curtain calls, 142
cutting, 8–9, 49, 52–53, 76, 88–91, 95, 99,
111, 127, 138, 141, 147, 151, 153, 160

dailies, 47, 160
Dallas, Tex., 6
Dancing with the Stars, 53
Danger, 24
Dark Electric Vision (Coppola), 3, 118
see also *Distant Vision* (Coppola); *Elective Affinities* (Coppola)
Days of Wine and Roses, 2, 24–25
Deadwood, 28
deafness, 18
Debussy, Claude, 30
Deer Hunter, The, 27
Denney, Mike, 131, 136, 138, 142, 151
dialects, 6
dialogue, 95, 141
Digidesign, 45–46
digital cameras, xii, 43, 74, 107–8, 112, 160
digital editing, 74, 110, 162
digital medium, xi–xii, 3, 14–15, 24,
29–30, 33–34, 107–8

digital settings, 54
digital television, 26, 160
directors:
action, 84
associate (ADs), 92–93, 95, 101–
2, 138, 159
film, xii, 3, 14–15, 24, 29–30,
33–34, 107–8
Internet, xii
in Live Cinema, 15–17, 24, 46,
92–93, 104–5
of photography (DPs), 160, 161
technical (TDs), 95, 101–2, 124, 130,
138, 144, 145–47, 152–53, 163–64
television, 2, 3, 11, 23–25, 30
theater, 3, 30
Disney, 12, 110
dissolves, 144
"distant electric vision," 18–20, 22
Distant Vision (Coppola), 59, 118, 122,
123, 124, 127–28, 129, 131, 135, 138,
155, 165–90
documentary films, 49–50
Dogville, 52, 53, 129
Dolby, Ray, 25
Dolce Vita, La, 116
Don Quixote (Cervantes), 123
doors, 57
Dowling, Robert M., 82
dramatic series, 26, 28
dress rehearsals, 34, 95, 99, 132, 133,
134–35, 160
Dumas, Alexandre, 82–83
DuMont Television Network, 2, 21, 23
Duvall, Robert, 38
Duvall, Shelley, 78

Eastman Kodak, xi–xii
Edison, Thomas, 20
editing:
cutting in, 8–9, 49, 52–53, 76, 88–91,
95, 99, 111, 127, 138, 141, 147,
151, 153, 160
digital, 74, 110, 162
final cuts in, 76, 111, 160
intercutting in, 95, 99
for Live Cinema, 46–47, 99, 104, 132
nonlinear, 45, 162
parallel, 21

editing (*continued*)
　sequences in, 141
　sound, 47, 70*n*, 99, 137, 141, 148,
　　160, 163–64
　video, 21
editorial assistants, 47
8½, 114, 116
8K cameras, 14–15, 160
8mm film, 108
Eisenstein, Sergei, 9, 88–91
Elective Affinities (Coppola), 72, 118
electricians, 161
electronic image screens, 54
electronic movie studios, 74
electronic signals, 159, 161
electrons, 159
elements, lighting, 58–59
emotional impact, 9, 10, 24–25, 50, 88–91
emulsion, xii
entertainment industry, 20, 106
entrances, 58, 86, 92
epilogues, 83
equalization, 45–46
establishing shots, 52–53, 133
Evans, Robert, 84
EVS ("ELVIS") DYVI switchers, 6,
　26, 44–47, 49, 60, 94, 95–99,
　103, 133, 135–36, 141, 143, 150,
　156, 160, 164
EVS XT3 replay servers, 45
exhibitions, 111–12
exits, 58, 86
experimental proof-of-concept workshops,
　see Oklahoma City Community
　College (OCCC) workshop; UCLA
　School of Theater, Film and Televi-
　sion workshop
exposure levels, 52
expressionism, 84, 85
exterior shots, 159
extras, 6, 94, 95, 99

FaceTime, 22
fades, 149, 151
Faerie Tale Theatre, 78–80
Fanny and Alexander, 113
Farnsworth, Philo, 19, 22
Fellini, Federico, 110, 113, 116
Few Good Men, A, 48

film, films:
　action, 54, 84
　animated, 11, 12, 51
　archival copies of, 118
　black and white, 113
　budgets for, 62, 70, 73, 85, 103
　celluloid or photochemical, xi–xii,
　　107–8, 109
　color, 113
　criticism and reviews of, 33–34,
　　69–70, 77, 79–80
　development and printing of, 107–8, 110
　documentary, 49–50
　8mm, 108
　grammar of, 9–12, 87–91
　invention of, 20
　lenses for, 12–13, 44, 108, 112
　masterpieces of, 112–14
　negatives of, 75
　one-shot, 29, 85
　preservation of, 110*n*, 113, 118
　production of, 5, 12, 21, 33, 76,
　　159–60, 163
　reels of, 22, 75, 102, 110, 111–12
　revenues from, 70, 72
　second units in, 61–62, 163
　silent, xi, 7, 21, 31, 87–88, 112–13
　16mm, 2, 21, 106–7
　sound ("talkies"), xi, 1, 21,
　　31–32, 47, 113
　soundtrack of, 47, 70–76
　studios for, 61, 73, 75, 112*n*
　subtitles in, 6, 99
　takes in, 85–86, 160
　televised, 12, 112
　35mm, 109–10, 111, 112
　3-D, 51, 109–10
　two-reel, 22
　Western, 2, 71
　see also cinema
Film Foundation, The, 113
film technicians, 160
final cuts, 76, 111, 160
final dress rehearsals, 132
Finian's Rainbow, 62
Flaherty, Joseph, 106–7
Flaherty, Robert J., 49–50
flashlights, 101
flat lenses, 13, 44, 52, 156

flat panels (Craig panels), 6, 55–59, 56, 86–87, 98, 163
flat screen television, 55
floor lamps, 13, 133
focal lengths, 162, 164
focus, 15, 162, 164
folding flaps, 60
Foley sounds, 99, 160
food, 38, 41, 94, 128, 129, 135
football games, 53, 85, 95, 156
foreign languages, 6, 99
formulas, 83
For Whom the Bell Tolls, 25
frame rate, 43–44, 93, 147, 161
frame rate converters, 44, 161
frame size, 160
framing, 155, 160
Frankenheimer, John, 2, 3, 24–25, 75
Frederickson, Gray, 5–6
"free spots," 133
French Connection, The, 28, 39
Friedkin, William, 39
Fuchs, Fred, 78
Funt, Allen, 105
furniture, 10, 34–35, 41, 129, 133, 145, 150

gaffers, 161
games, theater, xii, 34, 35, 36, 40–41, 128, 129, 142
gaming, xii
Gates, Bill, 74
Gayle, Crystal, 74
generator locking (genlock), 161
genres, 48, 84
Germany, 21–22, 117
Gershwin, George, 126n, 127, 150
Gerwig, Greta, 105
Glass Menagerie, The (Williams), 30
glass plates, xii
Gleason, Jackie, 28
glossary, 159–64
Godfather, The, 8–9, 36–37, 38, 70, 84
Godfather Part II, The, 70
Goethe, Johann Wolfgang von, 72, 108, 109, 113
Golden Age of Cinema, 61–62
Golden Age of Television, 2–3, 23–25, 27–28, 75, 93
Graham, Bill, 26–27

grammar, film, 9–12, 87–91
Grand Central Station, 23
graphic projections, 59
Grease Live!, 49, 111
Great Britain, 22
Greek theater, 83, 136
green screens, 46, 54, 55, 61, 85, 98, 132, 159–60
Gregory, Lady Augusta, 55–57
grid patterns, 85, 162
Griffith, D. W., 61
Gust, Anne, 66

Hackman, Gene, 39
hair styling, 94, 132, 134
Hamlet (Shakespeare), 55
ham radio, 95–97
handheld cameras, 54, 84–85, 161, 163
hand offs, 85
hand props, 35, 41
Handycam cameras, 108
Hanseatic League, 117
Harrelson, Woody, 29
Harvard University, 31
hats, 41
helical scan recorders, 25, 161
helicopters, 64, 73
hierarchical situations, 40
high-frequency signals, 161
Hitchcock, Alfred, 11, 21–22
Hollywood, 22, 25, 61–62, 69, 73, 74, 142, 143
Hollywood General Studios, 73
home theaters, 112
Honeymooners, The, 28
Horn & Hardart, 2
House of Wax, 109
Howdy Doody, 2
Hudson River Valley, 79
Hughie (O'Neill), 31

I Am Cuba, 85
Ibiza, 14–15
I Love Lucy, 25
improvisation, 34, 36–40, 41, 95, 128, 129
Independent Frame, 12, 133, 134
Industrial Revolution, 27
Inglenook (winery), 122
input/output routing, 46

Insdorf, Annette, 154
inserts, 140, 151
intercoms, 65–68, 92, 134, 136, 137, 138
intercutting, 95, 99
Internet, xii, 157, 161
Internet Protocol (IP), 161
Intolerance, 61
Inuit people, 49–50
iPads, 133
"IP Director" program, 99
Ishioka, Eiko, 78–79, 80
Italian language, 6, 99

Japan, 8, 107, 116
J. Arthur Rank studios, 12
Jesus Christ, 116
Jobs, Steve, 74
Jonze, Spike, 104
journalism, 7

Keaton, Buster, 33
Kerensky, Alexander, 91
Kinescope, 21, 161
Kinetograph, 20
King and I, The, 24
King of Comedy, The, 28
KMPX, 71
Kodak film, xi–xii
Kovacs, Ernie, 28
Kramer vs. Kramer, 70
Ku Klux Klan, 31
Kurosawa, Akira, 110, 113

Ladies Man, The, 75–76
lamps, 13, 52, 133, 162
Land, Edwin, 108–10
Lang, Fritz, 21
lasers, 109
Lasseter, John, 155
Las Vegas, 72–76, 141, 142, 152
Late Late Show, The, 53
lateness, 35–36
Laughton, Charles, 33
Laurie, Piper, 24–25
Lawrence of Arabia, 48–49, 69–70
Leachman, Cloris, 2
LED lights, 52, 54, 55, 98, 156
Leica viewfinders, 129
Lenin, Vladimir, 89, 89

lenses:
    adapters for, 44
    Bolex 16mm, 44
    C-mounts for, 44
    film, 12–13, 44, 108, 112
    flat, 13, 44, 52, 156
    focal lengths of, 162, 164
    lighting and, 12–13
    in television, 48
    zoom (telephoto), 12–13, 14, 48, 52,
        93, 162, 164
Lewis, Jerry, 75–76
LG Electronics, 55, 190
lighting:
    Appia effect in, 55, 59, 159
    arc, 111
    brightness of, 76, 160
    cinematic, 13, 52, 58–59, 76, 160
    cues for, 92, 132
    elements for, 58–59
    floor, 13, 133
    grids for, 12–13, 48, 52, 53, 101, 132, 133
    LED battery-powered, 52, 54, 55, 98, 156
    lenses and, 12–13
    mood and, 52
    opticals in, 144
    placement of, 86, 130, 132, 161
    practicals (set lamps) in, 52, 162
    projections of, 55, 58–59
    shadows and, 55, 159
    snoots (attachments) for, 52, 163
    theater, 55, 59, 81–82, 159
    ultraviolet (UV), 101
    uniform, 12–13
limited editions, 157
line rehearsals, 134
literature, 7–8, 9, 23–24, 113, 115–16
Little Fox Theater, 71
Live Cinema:
    acting in, xiii, 5–6, 7, 16, 29, 33–42,
        50–51, 86, 92, 93, 95–101, 104,
        105, 125, 126, 129, 134–35, 136,
        137, 139, 140, 144, 146, 150, 151,
        152, 154, 160
    animals in, 94, 95, 99
    audiences for, 7, 16, 30
    author's development of, xii–xiii,
        1–3, 15–17, 27, 34, 76, 77, 84,
        115–18, 121–57

behind-the-scenes preparations
for, 16–17
black cards for, 16–17
broadcasts of, 49, 103–5, 152
budgets for, 103
cameras in, 14, 15, 17, 43–44, 92–97,
110–11, 135
children in, 94, 95, 99
cinema compared with, 48, 85–86, 99,
103, 105, 111–12, 118
commercials in, 132, 146, 149, 151
as creative medium, xii–xiii, 113–14
credits for, xiii, 165–90
crew for, 17, 93, 95–97, 99, 119,
135, 160, 163
dialogue in, 95, 141
direction in, 15–17, 24, 46, 92–93, 104–5
editing in, 46–47, 99, 104, 132
emotional impact of, 9, 10, 50, 88–91
equipment for, xiii, 43–47, 106–14, 133
experimental proof-of-concept workshops for, see Oklahoma City Community College (OCCC) workshop;
UCLA School of Theater, Film and
Television workshop
extras in, 6, 94, 95, 99
games for, xii, 34, 35, 36, 40–41,
128, 129, 142
language of, 9–12
as live performance, xiii, 6, 11, 12,
15–17, 24, 28, 45–47, 50, 75, 76,
95–99, 103–5, 118, 130, 132–33, 138–
39, 140, 141, 156–57, 160
locations in, 48–62
makeup in, 94, 132, 143, 160
miscues in, 16
mixing in, 44–47, 98, 99, 136–37, 138,
139, 161, 162
obstacles in, 16, 101–5
performance standards in, 16–17,
29–32, 125, 132–34, 138–39, 140
pre-cut sequences in, 12, 15, 49, 60,
62, 87, 99
preparation and production for, 33–42,
85–87, 118, 154
pre-recording for, 16, 87, 94, 95, 99, 132,
135–36, 138
props for, 6, 10, 11–12, 16, 34–35, 41,
129, 130, 134, 135, 137

recording of, 49, 103–5, 118
rehearsals in, 33–42, 50–51, 92–97, 99,
129, 132, 133, 134–35, 163
scenery in, 48–62, 135, 137
scenes in, 34–35, 45, 93–95, 102, 130
screenplays (scripts) in, 3, 5–6, 35,
36, 42, 46–47, 59, 98, 115, 117–18,
127–28, 136
sets (scenery) for, 6, 10–11, 14, 15, 17,
46, 48, 51, 55–59, 56, 62, 86–87, 98,
128, 129, 139, 155
shots used in, 10, 11, 14, 50–53, 60–62,
87–91, 133
sound in, 47, 50, 126, 134, 136–
37, 148, 154
soundtracks in, 47, 70–76, 130, 132, 137,
138, 144, 145, 146, 147, 148
staging of, 34–35, 42, 60–62,
131, 145, 155
storyboards in, 11, 12, 46, 49, 163
storytelling in, 10, 11, 21
stunts in, 6, 95–97, 99
style of, 85–86, 132
supplementary sequences in, 87
takes in, 85–86
technical specifications for, 43–47,
133, 134, 135
television compared with, xii–xiii, 3,
10–11, 24, 28, 85–86, 118, 156
theater compared with, 34, 42, 76, 80,
86, 118, 139, 156
theatrical exhibitions of, 29, 111–12,
138, 156–57
three-act structure of, 41, 92
time manipulation in, 17, 49, 132,
139
time shifting for, 49
wardrobe in, 35, 41, 94, 132,
134, 137, 160
locations, 48–62
loop harnesses, 137
loops, sound, 137, 141, 148
Lorentz, Pare, 64
Los Angeles, 107, 121, 154
Lost in London, 29, 86, 111
love stories, 71
Lubitsch, Ernst, 21
Lucas, George, 69–70, 74, 156–57
Lumet, Sidney, 2, 24

Lumière, Auguste and Louis, 20
lunch breaks, 94, 128, 129
Lupino, Ida, 33

Macgowan, Kenneth, 32
MacGraw, Ali, 27
Mad Men, 28
magnetic tape recorders, 1, 161
Mahler, Gustav, 29–30
makeup, 94, 132, 143, 160
Malaimare, Mihai, Jr., 60
Manhattan, 28
manic depression, 155
Mann, Thomas, 116–17
marks, 99–101
married couples, 36
Marsyas, 136
Marty, 2, 24
Mason, James, 8
masterpieces, 112–14
master shots, 14–15, 53, 60, 150, 161
matrix boards, 161
McQueen, Steve, 70
meditation, 155
melodrama, 31
"memorable moments," 7
MGM, 73
microphones, 21, 136–37, 138
Microsoft, 74
Miller, JP, 24
minimalism, 85
miscues, 16
Mishima, 78–79
Mishima, Yukio, 78–79, 115–16
mixdowns, 162
mixing boards, 44–47, 98, 99, 136–37, 138,
    139, 161, 162
modular sets, 54, 55–59, 56, 86–87, 98
molded sets, 86
montage, 7, 9, 21, 87–91, 162
mood, 52
Moscow Art Theatre, 55
motion-control systems, 54, 162
Motorola television sets, 1
mounted cards, 93
"movie-movie" style, 84
multiviewers, 14, 45, 95, 102, 162
Murch, Walter, 70*n*
Murnau, F. W., 21, 110

music:
    classical, 1, 29–31, 68, 113, 114, 148
    cues for, 92
    instruments in, 114
    live, 99
    recording of, 137
"musical narrators," 74
musicals, 12, 26, 49, 70–76, 111
music-drama concept, 113
mute shows, 83
Muybridge, Eadweard, 20
My Life in Art (Stanislavski), 55

NAB Show, 106
Nanook of the North, 49–50
Napoleon I, Emperor of France, 91
narration, 74, 113
National Aeronautics and Space Adminis-
    tration (NASA), 66
National Association of Broadcasters
    (NAB), 106
National Football League (NFL), 53
naturalism, 85, 86
Nature, 18–19
Navajo carpets, 104
Nazism, 22
NBC, 1, 20, 47, 148
NBC Symphony Orchestra, 1
Neapolitan dialect, 99
Netflix, 84
networks, television, 2, 21, 25
news programs, 26, 28, 85
NewTek TriCaster, 43–44, 136, 137, 139
Newton, Isaac, 108
New York, N.Y., 1, 23, 24, 30–31, 154, 155
NHK, 107
nickelodeons, 21, 22
1950s, 116
Nobel Prize in Literature, 83
Nolan, Christopher, 107
nonlinear editing, 45, 162
novels, 7

obstacles, 16, 101–5
Obstfelder, Jürgen, 46
October (Ten Days That Shook the World),
    88–91, 89, 90
Oklahoma City Community College
    (OCCC) workshop, xiii, 3, 5–17,

33–44, 50, 51–53, 69, 98, 99, 103, 115, 118, 121–57, 165–73
Olivier, Laurence, 33
One from the Heart, 51, 66, 69–77, 77, 78, 111
O'Neill, Eugene, 31–32, 82–84, 117
O'Neill, James, 82–84, 82, 83
one-shot films, 29, 85
On Golden Pond, 10, 87
On the Art of the Theatre (Craig), 32
opera, 29, 30–31, 68, 113
operators, camera, 65–66, 101, 129, 138
Ophuls, Max, 7, 8
opticals, 144
orchestra, 114
Outsiders, The, 68
over-shoulder shots, 133
oversized props, 11–12
Ozu, Yasujiro, 7, 8, 110

Pabst, G. W., 21
Pacific Dome Theater, 69–70
Pacino, Al, 38
"package, the," 49
painted sets, 81–82
painting, 15
Palance, Jack, 2
panning, 111, 156
paparazzi, 116
paragraphs, 7
parallel editing, 21
Paramount Studios, 75
parody, 28
patents, 19, 22, 56, 58
Patsy's restaurant, 38
Patterns, 24
Patton, 70
Pelléas et Mélisande (Debussy), 30
Penn, Arthur, 2, 24
performance standards, 16–17, 29–32, 125, 132–34, 138–39, 140
Persian carpets, 104
perspective, 15
Peter Pan Live!, 156
Philco Television Playhouse, 2
phones, 112
photochemical film, xi–xii, 107–8, 109
photography, xii, 108–10
"Pick Up My Hat" theater game, 41

picture libraries, 61
Pinewood Studios, 12
Pixar, 51
pixel count, 160
Place in the Sun, A, 114
playback (PB), 141, 143, 145
Playhouse 90, 2, 25, 93, 107
Play-Making (Archer), 32
plays, xiii, 2–3, 9, 10, 23–25, 26, 48, 113
playwrights, 23–24
Plow That Broke the Plains, The, 64, 66
Polaroid, 108–10
Polaroid glasses, 109
Polaroid SK70 camera, 109
Polavision instant movie system, 108–10
political speeches, 62–68
post-production, 159–60
power cables, 52, 99, 124
practicals (set lamps), 52, 162
pre-designed shots, 12, 15, 49, 60, 62, 87, 99
presidential election campaign (1980), 63–68
press conferences, 142
Presto home acetate recorder, 1
pre-visualization, 51, 133, 134, 155, 162
printed sets, 86
prisons, 53
production designers, 76, 80
production period, 33–42, 85–87, 118, 154
productions:
    for cinema, 5, 12, 21, 33, 76, 159–60, 163
    for Live Cinema, 33–42, 85–87, 118, 154
    post-, 159–60
    for television, 106–7
    for theater, 34, 42, 76, 80
projections, light, 55, 58–59
projectors, 2, 74, 102, 109–12
pronunciation, 35
"proof of concept," 133
proof-of-concept workshops, *see* Oklahoma City Community College (OCCC) workshop; UCLA School of Theater, Film and Television workshop
props, 6, 10, 11–12, 16, 34–35, 41, 129, 130, 134, 135, 137
proscenium stages, 83

prose, 7
public domain material, 23
puppets, 2

radio, 1, 20
"Radio Row," 1
Raging Bull, 28
Rawnsley, David, 12, 133
Ray, Nicholas, 110
RCA, 19, 20, 22
read-throughs, 34, 35, 129
realism, 81–86
rear projection, 162
recording:
    audio, 1, 2, 21
    pre-, 16, 87, 94, 95, 99, 132, 135–36, 138
    video, xii, 2, 6, 21, 22, 25, 26, 75–76,
        106–7, 161
RED, 107
Red Desert, 113
reels, film, 22, 75, 102, 110, 111–12
rehearsals, 29, 33–42, 50–51, 55, 92–99,
    129, 132–39, 141, 160, 163
repertory theater, 5–6
replay signals, 46
reportage footage, 49–50
Requiem for a Heavyweight, 2, 24
reverse angle shots, 14, 60, 99
reviews, 33–34, 69–70, 77, 79–80
rhythmic measure, 47
Rich, Frank, 69
"Ride of the Valkyries" (Wagner), 68
Rimini, Italy, 144
"Rip Van Winkle," 78–80, 79
Robe, The, 61
Robertson, Cliff, 24–25
rock music, 31
role-playing games, xii, 34, 35, 36, 40–41,
    128, 129, 142
Rosing, Boris, 19, 22
rostrums, 12
Rozic, Teri, 46, 101–2, 124, 137, 138, 142
run-throughs, 34, 36–40, 93, 133, 134–35,
    138–39, 141, 163
Russian Ark, 29

Sabu, 73
salaries, 61
Samson and Delilah, 148

San Francisco News Letter, 82–83
Sarnoff, David, 20
satellites, 27, 62, 112
Saturday Night Live (SNL), 28–29
scenery (sets), 1, 6, 10–11, 14, 15, 17, 32,
    46, 48–62, 56, 57, 76, 81–87, 98,
    107, 128, 129, 135, 137, 138, 139,
    155, 162, 163
scenes, 9–10, 11, 34–35, 45, 54, 93–95,
    102, 130, 162
scenic design, 11, 32, 55–59, 56, 86–87,
    98, 107, 163
Schiller, Friedrich, 113
Schrader, Paul, 78–79
Schroeder, Barbet, 14–15
Schwartzman, Jason, 104
Scorsese, Martin, 113
scrims, 51–52
scripts (screenplays), 3, 5–6, 33–36, 42,
    46–47, 59, 71, 72, 75, 98, 99, 115,
    117–18, 127–28, 136
script supervisors, 99
second units, 61–62, 163
self-confidence, 35–36
sentences, 7–8, 9, 91
Sentinel Building, 71
seppuku (ritual suicide), 116
Serling, Rod, 2, 24
set lamps (practicals), 52, 162
sets (scenery), 1, 6, 10–11, 14, 15, 17, 32, 46,
    48–62, 56, 57, 76, 81–87, 98, 107, 128,
    129, 135, 137, 138, 139, 155, 162, 163
setups (camera placement), 29, 86, 99, 130,
    131, 139–40, 159
shadows, 55, 159
Shakespeare, William, 23, 55
Shape of Things to Come, The, 63–68, 65
Shire, Talia, 38, 84
shots:
    action, 88–91
    as basic units, 7–9, 10, 87
    as "bricks" or "building
        blocks," 8–9, 156
    cause-and-effect in, 88
    cinematic, 2–3, 13–14, 102
    close-up (CU), 10, 14, 15, 21, 32, 52–53,
        60, 88–89, 133, 146–47, 153–54, 161
    composition of, 8–9, 13–14, 86,
        88–91, 98, 134

concept of, 7–8
continuity of, 85, 135–36
coverage for, 10, 11, 12–13, 15, 48, 60,
    91, 133, 156, 160
creation and selection of, 11, 50–53,
    60–62, 130, 131, 132, 159
dissolves in, 144
dolly, 110–11, 148–49, 150, 160
dynamic, 89
editing of, *see* editing
establishing, 52–53, 133
exterior, 159
fades in, 149, 151
focus of, 15
footage quality of, 160
frame size of, 160
framing of, 155, 160
helicopter, 64, 73
insert, 140, 151
juxtaposition of (montage), 7, 9, 21,
    87–91, 162
in Live Cinema, 10, 11, 14, 50–53,
    60–62, 87–91, 133
location, 61–62
long, 10, 161
master, 14–15, 53, 60, 150, 161
medium, 10, 89
middle, 161
moving, 160
one, 85
optimal, 99
over-shoulder, 133
panning, 111, 156
perspective in, 15
pre-designed (pre-shoot), 12, 15, 49,
    60, 62, 87, 99
pre-visualization of (shot-by-shot), 51,
    133, 134, 155, 162
profile, 99
progressive, 88
reverse angle, 14, 60, 99
scenery in, 57
sequences of, 7, 162
side angle, 99
single continuous, 29, 85
staged, 49–50
Steadicam, 85, 110–11, 163
storyboards used in, 49, 163
succession of, 11

superimposition of, 88
television, 2–3, 11, 48
tracking, 8, 110–11, 160
transitional, 93–94
two-, 15
"weird angle," 32
wide, 88
wipes in, 153
as "words," 7–8, 9, 91
shutters, 161
side angle shots, 99
Signal Corps, U.S., 23
signal lights, 92
silent films, xi, 7, 21, 31, 87–88, 112–13
Sills, Paul, 35
"Silverfish, The," 66–68, 122, 123, 124,
    126, 128, 131, 135–36, 138, 140, 141,
    142, 143, 152
silver halides, xii
Singin' in the Rain, 114
16mm film, 2, 21, 106–7
16mm projectors, 2
60i (59.94 interlaced fields per sec-
    ond), 43, 44
Smith College, 109
snoots (light attachments), 52, 163
soap operas, 12, 52–53
software code, 46
soliloquies, 83
Song of Bernadette, The, 61
SONOS sound system, 154
Sony, 44, 107, 108
Sony Professional cameras, 107
Sony PXW-FS5 digital cameras, 44
Sony PXW-FS7 digital cameras, 44
Sopranos, The, 26, 28
sound:
    audio inputs for, 62
    collections of, 99, 102
    cues for, 137, 138, 141, 142
    design of, 99, 137, 160
    editing of, 47, 70n, 99, 137, 141, 148,
        160, 163–64
    effects in, 76, 99, 160
    equalization of, 45–46
    Foley, 99, 160
    in Live Cinema, 47, 50, 126, 134, 136–
        37, 148, 154
    loops in, 137, 141, 148

sound (*continued*)
  microphones for, 21, 136–37, 138
  mixing boards for, 45–46, 99, 138, 139
  playback (PB) in, 141, 143, 145
  recording of, 21, 99, 136–37, 138, 141, 143, 145
  stages for, 61–62
  synchronized, 47, 99, 163–64
  transmission of, 18
"Sound Ball" theater game, 40–41
sound films ("talkies"), xi, 1, 21, 31–32, 47, 113
sound rooms, 134
soundstages, 61–62
soundtracks, 47, 70–76, 130, 132, 137, 138, 144, 145, 146, 147, 148
special effects, 76, 86, 160, 162
Spielberg, Steven, 107
Spolin, Viola, 35, 40–41
sponsors, commercial, 20
sports, 9, 16, 17, 26, 43, 49, 50, 53, 84, 85, 94, 98, 107, 156
stagecraft, 60–61
stagehands, 55
stage managers, 92, 124, 138, 156
staging, 34–35, 42, 60–62, 82–84, 131, 145, 155
standing sets, 48
stand-ins, 155
Stanislavski, Konstantin, 55
Stanton, Harry Dean, 79
Star Wars, 54
stationary cameras, 54
stationary scenes, 54
Steadicam, 85, 110–11, 163
Steele, Tommy, 62
still photography, xii, 108–10
Storaro, Vittorio, 8, 9, 70*n*, 111
storyboards, 11, 12, 46, 49, 163
"story mode," 45
storytelling, 10, 11, 21, 26, 78–80
Strauss, Richard, 29–30
Streetcar Named Desire, A (Williams), 30
Strindberg, August, 113
studios, film, 61, 73, 75, 112*n*
stumble-throughs, 34, 92–97
stunts, 6, 95–97, 99
subtitles, 6, 99
synchronization, 47, 99, 163–64

tablets, 112
"talkies" (sound films), xi, 1, 21, 31–32, 47, 113
tally lights, 93, 163
tape recorders, 1, 2, 21
Tarantino, Quentin, 107
Tavoularis, Dean, 76
Taxi Driver, 28
technical directors (TDs), 95, 101–2, 124, 130, 138, 144, 145–47, 152–53, 163–64
technology:
  broadcast, 1–2, 25, 106–7
  camera, 14–15, 21, 43, 44, 60, 107, 160
  computer, 44, 46, 112, 157
  cost of, 106
  digital, 26, 107
  electronic, 18–20, 22
  film, 113–14
  rehearsals for, 95, 99
  specifications for, 43–47, 133, 134, 135
  television, xii, 18–20, 25–26, 106–7
"Telegraphic Photography and Electric Vision" (Bidwell), 18–19
telephones, 18
telephoto lenses, 12–13, 14, 48, 52, 93, 162, 164
television:
  actors in, 23, 24
  audiences for, 105
  broadcasts of, 1–2, 25, 106–7
  budgets of, 64
  cable, 28
  cameras for, 43, 75, 93
  cathode ray tubes (CRTs) in, 19, 21, 159
  cinema compared with, 2–3, 12, 23, 24–28, 78, 112
  comedy series on, 28–29
  commercials on, 20
  cultural impact of, 20, 106, 116–17, 131, 143
  development of, 1–2
  digital, 26, 160
  as "distant electric vision," 18–20, 22
  dramatic series on, 26, 28
  editing for, 21, 22
  electric and electronic, 18–20, 22
  emotional impact of, 24–25
  events in, 9, 10, 86, 107, 156

executives in, 52–53
films shown on, 12, 112
first golden age of, 23–25
flat screen, 55
Golden Age of, 2–3, 23–25,
    27–28, 75, 93
history of, 18–32
instant replay servers in, 6, 26
invention of, xii, 18–20
lenses used in, 48
lighting grids (overhead lighting) in,
    12–13, 48, 52, 53, 101, 132, 133
literary adaptations for, 23–24
live, xii, xiii, 2–3, 11, 21, 24–25, 26,
    62–66, 78–80, 85, 93, 133, 161, 162
Live Cinema compared with, xii–xiii, 3,
    10–11, 24, 28, 85–86, 118, 156
mechanical, 18, 20
name of (Tele-Vision), 20
networks for, 2, 21, 25
news programs on, 26, 28, 85
patents for, 19, 22
picture quality for, 22
plays on, xiii, 2–3, 9, 10, 23–25,
    26, 48, 113
production for, 106–7
programming of, 1–3, 20
props for, 11–12
recording of, 21, 22, 25, 106–7, 161
screen boxes in, 85
second golden age of, 27–28
sets for, 1, 10
shots used in, 2–3, 11, 48
sports programs on, 9, 16, 17, 26, 43, 49,
    50, 53, 84, 85, 94, 98, 107, 156
storytelling in, 26, 78–80
studios for, 106–7
style of, 2–3, 9, 12–15, 20, 24–25, 85
switchers in, 45–46
technology of, xii, 18–20, 25–26, 106–7
time shifting in, 21, 49
tenements, 59
Terry, Ellen, 55
test patterns, 1–2
Tetro, 39–40
textured sets, 86
t-handles, 163–64
theater:
    actors in, 3, 5–6, 10, 34

audiences for, 9–10, 30–31
casting in, 34
cinema compared with, 31–32, 83, 84
design in, 76, 80
games for, xii, 34, 35, 36, 40–41,
    128, 129, 142
Greek, 83, 136
history of, 31–32
lighting in, 55, 59, 81–82, 159
Live Cinema compared with, 34, 42,
    76, 80, 86, 118, 139, 156
meta-, 139
music cues in, 92
in New York (Broadway), 23, 24, 30–31
performances in, 86
plays in, xiii, 2–3, 9, 10, 23–25, 26, 48, 113
production of, 34, 42, 76, 80
realism in, 81–84
rehearsals in, 34, 42, 55
repertory, 5–6
scenes in, 9–10, 11
sets (scenery) in, 46, 48, 55–59, 56,
    81–82, 83, 85, 86–87, 98
staging in, 82–84
television compared with, xiii, 2–3, 9,
    10, 23–25, 26, 48, 78
ticket prices for, 30–31
touring in, 23, 82–83
in U.S., 82–84, 117
Theater Games for Rehearsal
    (Spolin), 35, 40–41
Theatre of Tomorrow, The (Macgowan), 32
theatrical exhibitions, 29, 111–12,
    138, 156–57
theremins, 114
Thief of Baghdad, The, 73
30p (standard TV frame rate), 93
35mm film, 109–10, 111, 112
This Property Is Condemned, 23n
three-act structure, 41, 92
3-D films, 51, 109–10
tilting, camera, 111, 149–50
Time, 69
time manipulation, 17, 49, 132, 139
time shifting, 21, 49
time signatures, 47
Toscanini, Arturo, 1, 148
Toshiba, 25
tracking shots, 8, 110–11, 160

Translight screens, 54, 55, 61
Traviata, La (Verdi), 29, 30, 111
triangulating, 54
tripods, 161
Tristan und Isolde (Wagner), 30
Turner, Ted, 26
Turn of the Screw, The, 25
12 Angry Men, 10, 87
20th Century Fox, 61–62
24p (23.98 progressive frames per second), 43–44
two-color photography, 108
two-reel films, 22

UCLA School of Theater, Film and Television workshop, xiii, 3, 14, 15–17, 33–42, 46, 50, 54–62, 69, 85, 93, 95–97, 98, 99, 102, 103, 115, 118, *119*, 121, 174–89
UFA GmbH, 21–22
ultraviolet (UV) light, 101
uniform lighting, 12–13
University of California at Los Angeles (UCLA), 75

vacuum-formed sets, 86
vacuum tubes, 159
Verdi, Giuseppe, 29, 30, 111, 113
Victoria, 29
Vidal, Gore, 24
video:
    cameras for, 106–7, 110
    editing of, 21
    effects in, 79–80
    mixing boards for, 45–46, 163–64
    multiple sources of, 161
    recorders (playback), xii, 2, 6, 21, 22, 25, 26, 75–76, 106–7, 161
    streaming, 44–47, 95–99, 135–36
    switchers for, 6, 26, 44–47, 49, 60, 94, 95–99, 103, 133, 135–36, 141, 143, 150, 156, 160, 164
videotape, xii, 2, 106–7
Vietnam War, 77, 115, 116
viewfinders, 75, 129
virtual reality, xii
Vishnevetsky, Ignatiy, 79–80
visualization, 51

Vitaphone, 1
voiceovers, 134
von Trier, Lars, 52

Wagner, Richard, 29–30, 68, 113
Waits, Tom, 74
Walküre, Die (Wagner), 68
walls, 60
Wanamaker's department store, 23
wardrobe, 35, 41, 94, 132, 134, 137, 160
Warner Bros., 62
Way of Chinese Painting, The, 15
weather conditions, 64–65, 163
"weird angle" shots, 32
Weiss, Craig, 155
Westerns, 2, 71
West Side Story, 30
Williams, Tennessee, 30
Willis, Gordon, 8–9
windows, 13, 57
Wine Spectator, 122
wipes, 153
Wire, The, 28
wire recorders, 1
Wisconsin State Capitol, 63–68
word processing, 47
words, 7–8, 9, 47, 91
workshops, *see* Oklahoma City Community College (OCCC) workshop; UCLA School of Theater, Film and Television workshop
World War II, 23
writing, 7–8, 47
Wyler, William, 110

Xerox PARC, 74
Xerox Star computers, 73–74

Yale School of Drama, 23, 31
Yeats, William Butler, 55–57
Young and the Restless, The, 53
YouTube Music Awards, 104

Zegel, Barry, 107
Zoetrope Studios, 66, 71–73, 76, 80, 189
zoom lenses, 12–13, 14, 48, 52, 93, 162, 164
Zworykin, Vladimir, 19, 22

ABOUT THE AUTHOR

Francis Ford Coppola is best known as the six-time Academy Award–winning director of such films as the *Godfather* trilogy and *Apocalypse Now*. Born in Detroit in 1939, Coppola grew up in Queens, New York. Paralyzed by polio as a child, he wrote stories and developed an interest in film after being given a toy movie projector.

A prolific theater and film student at Hofstra College and UCLA, he wrote short stories and plays (considering himself first and foremost a writer), and throughout his career has endeavored to write and direct original work. He made his mark as the Oscar-winning screenwriter of *Patton* in 1970, and followed it up in the rest of the '70s by writing, directing, and/or producing *The Godfather*, *The Godfather Part II*, *American Graffiti*, *The Conversation*, and *Apocalypse Now*, resulting in two Cannes Palme d'Or Awards, twelve Academy Award nominations, and five Academy Awards, making the period arguably the most successful decade any filmmaker has ever had.

Francis has also been producing wine for over thirty-five years at his Napa Valley and Sonoma Valley wineries. His other business interests include luxury resorts in Central America, Argentina, and

Italy, and an award-winning short story magazine, *Zoetrope: All-Story*. Francis's current passion is a new form of art he calls *Live Cinema*, being a combination of theater, film, and television. He is presently working on a cycle of screenplays he hopes to produce in this new medium.